THE ARCHITECTURE OF RICHARD NEUTRA: FROM INTERNATIONAL STYLE TO CALIFORNIA MODERN

ARTHUR DREXLER AND THOMAS S. HINES

THE MUSEUM OF MODERN ART, NEW YORK

To Henry
Here's to you
Thank you for
your Beekee...
Sept 1 82

Copyright © 1982 by
The Museum of Modern Art
All rights reserved
Library of Congress Catalog Card
Number 82-81426
ISBN 0-87070-506-7
Designed by Keith Davis
Typeset by Concept Typographic
Services, Inc., New York
Printed and bound by The Murray Printing
Company, Westford, Mass.

The Museum of Modern Art
11 West 53 Street
New York, New York 10019

Printed in the United States of America

Cover photograph: Richard Neutra.
Singleton house, Los Angeles, 1959.
Photograph by Julius Shulman.

The exhibition of Richard Neutra's architecture this catalog accompanies should help to further that process of "reappraisal" by which a neglected achievement will find a just estimate of its worth. At the Museum the reappraisal of Neutra's architecture began when the Department of Architecture and Design, through a generous grant from the Best Products Company, was enabled to enlarge its collection of architectural models. Although the collection included some thirty models representing major buildings of the modern movement, there was no model of any building by Richard Neutra. This was the first deficiency the Department wanted to remedy, and the obvious choice was Neutra's Lovell house of 1927-29.

When the new Lovell house model was shown for the first time in the Museum's 1979 exhibition "Art of the Twenties," it became a subject of animated discussion for the general public as well as for the architects and students who crowded around it. Their interest confirmed the Department's conclusion: Richard Neutra's architecture had been too long neglected and the time had come for an exhibition of his work.

Thomas S. Hines, Professor, Department of History and School of Architecture and Urban Planning at the University of California, Los Angeles, where he has been Faculty Advisor to the Neutra Archive established in 1955, has collaborated with me as codirector of the Museum's Neutra exhibition. At the time we first discussed this project, Mr. Hines was working on a book called *Richard Neutra and the Search for Modern Architecture: a Biography and History,* in which he examines Neutra's complex personality and his contribution to the development of a new architecture in a specifically American context. Publication of Mr. Hines' book by Oxford University Press coincides with the opening of the exhibition. For this catalog Mr. Hines has provided an extensive chronology of Neutra's life and work. The two publications complement each other: since we agreed that Neutra's houses, beginning with work of the late twenties and continuing into the sixties, are by far his most significant buildings, the exhibition and this catalog concentrate on houses. My own essay examines, among other things, Neutra's development of design details that are the equivalents of classical Japanese motifs.

I am grateful to Mr. Hines for putting his wide knowledge of Neutra's work at our disposal, and also for arranging the loan of some seventy-five original drawings from the Neutra Archive. In this regard, and on behalf of the Museum, I wish to thank James Mink, Director, and Brooke Whiting, Curator, of the Department of Special Collections of the University Research Library at UCLA for releasing these drawings for an extended period of time.

We are especially grateful to the architect's wife, Dione Neutra, and to the architect's son and professional associate, Dion Neutra, for their unstinting helpfulness. Mrs. Neutra's sister, Regula Niedermann Fybel, very kindly agreed to lend to the exhibition the portrait drawing of her reproduced on page 26. Theodore R. Gamble, Jr., has generously enabled us to commission a model of Neutra's Landfair apartment house.

Beginning in 1932, the Department of Architecture and Design had accumulated quite an extensive photographic file of Neutra's work, and this has been supplemented by additional material generously provided by Dion Neutra. The various photographers whose pictures first made Neutra's architecture known internationally are credited elsewhere in this catalog, but it is necessary here to single out Julius Shulman. More than half of the photographs in this publication are his, and it may accurately be said that in his often dramatic interpretations we see Neutra's buildings exactly as Neutra wanted them to be seen.

I am always grateful to Mary Jane Lightbown for her help in organizing materials for both the catalog and the exhibition, and I am indebted to Marie-Anne Evans for her skill in preparing manuscripts. Susan Weiley's editorial services have been especially helpful, and Keith Davis has brought order and clarity to the catalog.

Arthur Drexler
Director of Architecture and Design
The Museum of Modern Art

This exhibition is sponsored in part by a grant from the National Endowment for the Arts.

CONTENTS

1892

■ April 8: Richard Joseph Neutra born at Josephinengasse 7, Second District, Vienna, the third son and fourth child of Samuel and Elizabeth (Glazer) Neutra. His father owns a small foundry, casting machine parts for the city of Vienna.

1894

■ Neutra family moves to a larger apartment at Taborstrasse 72, near the Augarten, a great public park, which Richard remembers as his favorite childhood place.

1898

■ Autumn: Enters Second District Primary School, which he attends for four years.

1902

■ Autumn: Enters Sophiengymnasium, Zirkusgasse 46. Favorite classes are history and biology.

1910

■ Passes final gymnasium examinations "with distinction." In "Austrian Studies," speaks on "Austrian princes as patrons of art and science."

■ Begins a sporadically kept diary, noting major cultural and social interests and activities. Becomes enamored of poet Rainer Maria Rilke, philosopher Friederich Nietzsche, dramatists Arthur Schnitzler and Hugo von Hofmannsthal, painter Gustav Klimt, composers Gustav Mahler and Arnold Schönberg, and architects Otto Wagner and Adolf Loos. With brothers Wilhelm, a physician, and Siegfried, an attorney, sister Josephine, an artist, and brother-in-law Arpad Weixilgärtner, a curator at the Kunsthistorisches Museum, Neutra begins to experience the cultural richness of Vienna.

■ Walking and sketching trip through Bohemia and Franconia.

■ Autumn: Begins year of obligatory military service in the army reserve.

1911

■ Autumn: Enters four-year architecture program at Vienna Technische Hochschule, where he is particularly influenced by professors Rudolf Saliger, Karl Mayreder, and Max Fabiani.

1912

■ Walking and sketching trips of Italy and the Balkans with school friend Ernst Freud, son of Sigmund Freud. Produces beautiful pencil, crayon, and watercolor travel sketches. Later in the year vacations with the Freud family in the Tyrol.

■ Autumn: In his second year at Technische Hochschule, he enters studio-salon of Adolf Loos. Enjoys social meetings with Loos and his circle at the Kärtner Bar, absorbs his enthusiasm for America, and joins Loos on inspection visits to his Steiner and Scheu houses. In Loos's studio meets Rudolph Schindler.

1914

■ Discovers the work of Frank Lloyd Wright in the German Wasmuth edition of Wright's oeuvre. Resolves with the encouragement of Loos and Schindler "to go to the places where he walked and worked" and to see his "houses for people in another world."

■ Schindler leaves in January to join an office in Chicago with hopes of eventually working for Wright. He and Neutra begin an intense correspondence comparing the new world with the old and discussing their plans and goals for a life in architecture. Neutra intends to join him in 1915, after completing his degree at the Technische Hochschule, but is thwarted by the outbreak of war in 1914.

■ June: Called to active military duty as an artillery lieutenant and sent to Trebinje, Serbia, on the Balkan front after assassination of Austrian Archduke Franz Ferdinand makes war appear imminent.

1915

■ Monitors movements of enemy ships along the Adriatic coast and experiences sporadic inland skirmishes with Serbian partisans.

■ Designs Officers' Tea House, his first constructed building, a modest, partially open shelter that primitively anticipates his lifelong penchant for post-and-beam pavilions.

1916

■ Hospitalized with acute malaria and incipient tuberculosis.

1917

■ Sufficiently recovered from illnesses to return to Vienna to complete school, though not well enough to return to active duty. Continues to enjoy the cultural riches of Vienna. With Josephine and Arpad Weixilgärtner visits Gustav Klimt and other luminaries of the art world.

1918

■ Completes course of study at Technische Hochschule and on July 26 passes final examination with a mark of "excellent." Recurrent malaria prevents his returning to active duty, and he retires to nursing home in Trêncin, Slovakia, where on November 11 he learns of the Armistice.

1919

■ Returns briefly to Vienna and then moves to Stäfa, Switzerland, near Zurich, to Elsa Telekey's Erholungsheim, a rest home recommended by army friends. Finds work as an apprentice to Gustav Ammann in Otto Froebel's nursery in Zurich. Participates in studio of Karl Moser at Zurich Technische Hochschule and accompanies class on sketching expeditions.

■ At Erholungsheim meets Alfred Niedermann and his eleven-year-old granddaughter, Regula, who invite him to visit in the Niedermann home nearby. There he meets Regula's eighteen-year-old sister, Dione, who in 1922 will become his wife.

■ September: Joins the small architectural office of Wernli & Staeger in Wädenswil, Switzerland. His low regard for his unprogressive employers, the bitterly cold winter of 1919-20, the painful memories of the war years, the anti-Semitism he experiences, and Dione's absence in Vienna send him into prolonged depression. Longs to join friend Rudolph Schindler, soon to be working for Wright in "sunny California."

1920

■ Called home to Vienna in the early spring to see his dying father and rejoins Dione, who is there studying music. Becomes engaged. Decides not to return to Wernli & Staeger and finds temporary work in Vienna as interpreter and researcher with the American Friends Service Mission.
■ With the help of school friend Ernst Freud, now practicing architecture in Berlin, gets job in the office of Pinner & Neumann and in October moves to the German capi-

Neutra, ca. 1919, Switzerland, in Austrian army uniform.

tal. Soon dismissed when a big commission expected by the firm fails to materialize. Works part-time as theater extra and assistant to a lampmaker.

1921

■ Finds work in the architectural office of Heinrich Staumer. Applies for, and is awarded, position of city architect in nearby town of Luckenwalde. Designs public housing complex, in a chastened version of a gemütlich German folk idiom, and a municipally sponsored forest cemetery, which includes entrance gate, chapel, and administrative and maintenance structures. Their style reflects Neutra's efforts to fuse official building standards with modernist Wagnerschule and Prairie School elements.
■ Autumn: Hears of opening in Berlin office of Erich Mendelsohn and is hired on the strength of one interview. Assists on the landscaping of Mendelsohn's Einstein Tower in Potsdam and the design and execution of renovations and additions to the *Berliner Tageblatt* offices of the Mosse Verlag.

1922

■ Develops with Mendelsohn the winning, though unexecuted, design for a commercial center in Haifa, Palestine: plain, low-slung concrete buildings, accented chiefly by long bands of ribbon windows and crisply cantilevered balconies. Collaborates on a stylistically similar group of detached houses for the developer Adolf Sommerfeld, completed the following year in the Berlin suburb of Zehlendorf.

Neutra and Mendelsohn. Zehlendorf houses, Berlin, 1923.

■ Marries Dione during the Christmas holidays in Hagen, Westphalia, to which city the Niedermann family has moved. Couple returns to live in Berlin.

1923

■ Although stimulated and edified by his work in Mendelsohn's office, continues efforts to obtain visa to the United States. The Austro-American peace treaty, signed in August, helps clear the way. Sails on October 13. Arrives in New York on October 24. Dione stays behind with her parents in Hagen to await the birth of their first child.
■ Autumn: Rents a room in the small apartment of old Viennese school friend Henry Menkes. Works briefly for architects C. W. Short and Maurice Courland. Prepares a design at the request of an American Zionist group for a library of Jewish culture in Jerusalem. Design reflects motifs from Wright's Mason City, Iowa, hotel and Gropius's Cologne Werkbund building, though the library commission is ultimately won by others. Enjoys exploring and observing the great "accidental beauty" of New York.

1924

■ January 6: Son is born and named for Frank Lloyd Wright.
■ Late February: Leaves New York and arrives in Chicago, which strikes him as "as a fat, dirty, healthy child with great potential." James Forrestal, a Chicago Quaker acquaintance encountered earlier in Vienna, helps him secure temporary lodging at Jane Addams's Hull House. Later moves to an apartment in the north Chicago suburb of Highland Park.
■ Early March: Secures a job as draftsman no. 208 in the old, prestigious firm of Holabird & Roche. Works exclusively on the design and supervision of the building of the Palmer House Hotel.
■ Spring: Visits all of Sullivan's and Wright's buildings. Calls on Louis Sullivan, who is

dying in poverty and neglect in a south Chicago hotel, and discusses the history and the future of modern architecture. At Sullivan's funeral in late April meets Frank Lloyd Wright, who invites him to visit Taliesin.

■ June: Returns to New York to meet Dione, arriving from Europe, and has coincidental reunion with Schindler, who is in New York on business. Remarks of Schindler that "after ten years separation, we were not disappointed in each other."

■ Early July: Richard and Dione visit Taliesin, Spring Green, Wisconsin, which impresses them more than anything they have seen so far in America. Neutra resigns position with Holabird & Roche after Wright offers him a job, and moves to Taliesin in early November. Works on several of Wright's ultimately unbuilt projects, of which most significant is a drive-in recreation tower for Sugarloaf Mountain, Maryland. Enjoys the rural Wisconsin life, which is enlivened by visits from Erich Mendelsohn; Wright's oldest son, Lloyd; and Olgivanna Lazovich, later to become Wright's third wife.

1925

■ Early February: Leaves Wisconsin and moves to Los Angeles. Rents apartment in Schindler's house and studio on Kings Road. Works with Schindler on several projects, including a pool and pergola for Aline Barnsdall's estate in Hollywood, the project that in 1920 had first brought Wright and Schindler to Los Angeles. Supplements income by working for other more established architects, including the eclectic traditionalist Gordon Kaufman. Enjoys exploring Southern California and discovering, in particular, Irving Gill's abstract early twentieth-century interpretations of Spanish Colonial architecture.

1926

■ A second son, Dion, is born, though the happiness of this event is marred by the Neutras' growing realization that their oldest child, Frank, is mentally retarded as a result of a birth defect.

■ In these lean years without commissions, Neutra continues to design the elements of his ideal metropolis—Rush City Reformed, a name coined to evoke the fast pace of American life and the boom towns of legend. The Spartan geometry of its regularly spaced skyscraper slabs recalls the urban visions of the Italian Futurists, Le Corbusier, and Ludwig Hilbersheimer, although the contrasting areas of organically sprawling low-rise housing, shops, and schools suggest the less densely packed landscapes of Los Angeles.

■ Completes his first book, published the next year as *Wie Baut Amerika? (How America Builds),* discussing the problems and celebrating the possibilities of American architecture and urban design. Uses his experience with Holabird & Roche's Palmer House in Chicago as his chief example of high-rise construction and the concrete

Top: **Ring Plan School, 1926-27.** *Bottom:* **Rush City Reformed, 1926-27.**

California buildings of Schindler and the Wrights as examples of smaller structures in "sensitive conformity to the landscape." Book is widely reviewed and praised.

■ Does the minimal landscaping for Schindler's stylistically advanced beach house for Philip and Leah Lovell, at Newport Beach, California. Lovell is a naturopath physician whose column "Care of the Body" in the *Los Angeles Times* advocates vigorous exercise, natural methods of healing, and abstinence from drugs, alcohol, and tobacco.

■ Persuades Schindler to join him in the design of a submission to the League of Nations competition. The curving Mendelsohnian forms of the early preliminaries of the main facade give way in the final version to rectilinear, cantilevered, overhanging balconies. The design fails to win a prize, but is selected, along with the submissions of Le Corbusier and Hannes Meyer, for a traveling exhibition sponsored by the German Werkbund. Dione's father, Alfred Niedermann, handling the team's negotiations in Europe, decides that his son-in-law has done "the lion's share" of the work and blithely omits Schindler's name from the entry. Schindler's dismay at this action strains his and Neutra's relationship.

■ The desire and penchant for large-scale enterprises that had motivated Neutra to do the League of Nations design prompts the formation of a partnership with Schindler to be called the Architecture Group for Industry and Commerce (AGIC). Few of the groups' ambitious projects will ever be built, the major exception being the Jardinette Apartments, Los Angeles (1927), largely designed by Neutra and constituting his first important building in America. It is one of the first "pure" examples in the United States of what will come to be called "the International Style." Its four-story, U-shaped plan contains fifty-five apartments in a stark, poured-concrete structure

7

of cantilevered balconies and long, continuous window bands. Critic-historian Henry-Russell Hitchcock finds it "as fine and as modern as any of [the contemporary] German work."

1927

■ Commissioned by Schindler's former client, Philip Lovell, to design a great house for him and his family in Los Angeles. Schindler will later claim that Neutra "took" the commission from him; Neutra, that Lovell gave him the commission because of personal and professional dissatisfaction with Schindler.

1928-29

■ Designs and supervises the building of the epochal Lovell "Health" House, a three-story steel, glass, and concrete residence, entered from the top and perched dramatically on a steep hillside site. It is the first documented steel-framed house in America and, after the more primitive Jardinette Apartments, the first mature example in the country of the International Style. Its great southwestern facade epitomizes the aesthetic of machine assemblage. Lovell house becomes quickly and widely acclaimed.

Jardinette Apartments, Los Angeles, 1927.

1929

■ Teaches course in architecture at the Los Angeles Academy of Modern Art. Students include future architects Gregory Ain and Harwell Harris, photographers Willard and Barbara Morgan, and painter Anita Delano. Design and construction of Lovell Health House used as a pedagogical case study.

1930

■ Returns to Europe via Japan, China, the Indian Ocean, and the Suez Canal. In Japan he meets Kunio Maekawa and is moved and delighted by Japanese architecture. In Germany he meets Alvar Aalto, Walter Gropius, and Ludwig Mies van der Rohe; Mies invites him to the Bauhaus, where he teaches for a month as a visiting critic. In Rotterdam he visits Brinkman and Van der Vlugt's modern home and factory for C. H. Van der Leeuw, and attends, as the American delegate, the Brussels meeting of the Congres Internationaux d'Architecture Moderne (CIAM). There he meets Le Corbusier, who joins him on a visit to Josef Hoffmann's Stoclet House.

■ Publishes *Amerika: Neues Bauen in der Welt* ("America: New Building in the World"), which continues to extoll American building practices and introduces to a European public such relatively unknown architects as Irving Gill.

1931

■ Visits New York, lectures at the New School for Social Research, and is commissioned by Homer Johnson, the father of Philip, on behalf of ALCOA and the White Motors Company of Cleveland, to design an all-aluminum bus. Neutra moves temporarily to Cleveland, where he is paid a handsome fee in the early Depression years to design the buses, which are ultimately not produced.

■ Returns to Los Angeles. Rents bungalow on Douglas Street, Echo Park district, as home and studio. Student apprentices Har-

ris, Ain, and Raphael Soriano assist on various, ultimately unbuilt, projects.

1932

■ Neutra is featured, along with Mies, Gropius, Oud, Le Corbusier, Wright, and others, in the epoch-making "Modern Architecture" show at The Museum of Modern Art, which curators Philip Johnson and Henry-Russell Hitchcock label "the International Style" because of "its simultaneous development in several different countries and because of its worldwide distribution." Neutra's Zehlendorf houses, Jardinette Apartments, Lovell Health House, and Ring Plan School are exhibited to document his work. Museum director Alfred Barr calls him, principally because of his writings, "among American architects ... second only to Wright in his international reputation" and "the leading modern architect of the West Coast." After leaving New York the show travels to eleven other American cities, including Los Angeles. When the Los Angeles County Museum of Art refuses to exhibit it, Neutra persuades Bullocks-Wilshire Department Store to present it in the new store's gallery. The show is widely acclaimed and helps to confirm Neutra's burgeoning reputation.

■ Designs small, modern, flat-roofed "bungalow" in the International Housing Exhibition sponsored by the city of Vienna and the Austrian Werkbund in the Viennese suburb of Lainz. Other model houses by Adolf Loos, Josef Hoffmann, André Lurçat, Gerrit Rietveld, and Hugo Häring. Unlike its more famous predecessor at Stuttgart-Weissenhof (1927), which had emphasized apartments, the Vienna exhibition emphasizes attached and detached single-family houses.

■ Office building for Carl Laemmle and Universal-International Pictures completed at the celebrated corner of Hollywood and Vine, Los Angeles. Ground floor contains small street-front shops and the Coco Tree restaurant. Above the second-floor offices

Top: **House, Austrian Werkbund Exhibition, Vienna, 1932.** *Center:* **Mosk house, Los Angeles, 1933.** *Bottom:* **Laemmle/Universal-International Building, Los Angeles, 1932-33.**

are vast, integrally designed billboards advertising Universal's films. A tall and dramatically modern clock articulates the corner entrance. Rear service yard is a crisp essay in elegant minimalism.

■ With a low-interest loan from Dutch industrialist, philanthropist, and architectural enthusiast C. H. Van der Leeuw, Neutra builds a house/studio for himself and his family on Silverlake Reservoir in north-central Los Angeles. Lower floor contains office, drafting rooms, and small residential apartment. Second floor, topped by a roof-deck solarium, houses family living quarters. A stark, handsome, modular, white stucco building, with banded casement windows and silver-gray trim, utilizing the latest industrialized building materials, the structure is named the Van der Leeuw Research House in honor of its benefactor.

1933

■ Designs Mosk house, Hollywood, Los Angeles, for a young couple of modest income fervently dedicated to modernism. Planned as a replicable prototype for "a steep hillside development." The other units of this development are never built, though variants are realized in Neutra's housing projects of the later thirties and forties. The flat-roofed, ribbon-windowed wood and stucco house, painted silver-gray to suggest its "machine" identity, is enlivened by pergolas and cornice bands that extend beyond the house toward nature and infinity.

1934

■ Designs a small house in the Hollywood Hills of Los Angeles for the eccentric German-American art collector Galka Scheyer, a patron of the "Blue Four" German painters: Jawlensky, Kandinsky, Klee, and Feininger. Scheyer chooses Neutra above her closer friends Schindler and J. R. Davidson because she wants "the most modern" architect and believes Neutra is that. The major feature of the tiny house is a gallery/studio/living room where the Blue Four paintings hang.

■ Designs all-metal Beard house, Altadena, California, constructed of "cellular elements, approximating a series of vertical flues side by side, with vertical air intakes and automatically self-cooling exterior walls." The son of the Neutras' close friends, historians Charles and Mary Beard, William Beard is a professor of engineering at Cal Tech. His wife, Melba, is an aviator. As such, they typify the adventurous modernist clients, eager to build not only a beautiful and comfortable house, but one that demonstrates experimental and replicable technological possibilities. House wins 1934 Gold Medal of the "Better Homes in America" competition, cosponsored by *Architectural Forum* and the Columbia Broadcasting System.

■ Designs large, two-story white stucco house with silver-gray trim for actress Anna Sten and her husband, producer Eugene Frenke, in Santa Monica Canyon, Los Angeles, overlooking the ocean. Frosted glass stairwell fenestration and curving "winter garden" extension of living room predict recurring Neutra trademarks. First modern house to win first prize in annual *House Beautiful* competition.

1935

■ Von Sternberg house, Northridge, California, for the noted German-American film director. The house itself is a simple rectangular two-story structure. Its interest and significance comes from certain "special effects" Neutra gives to the design: the curving wall around the front patio; the high, screenlike wall dividing front and rear gardens; and the system of shallow "moats" encircling the house. Von Sternberg sells the house in the mid-1940s, and it is ultimately acquired by the novelist Ayn Rand. It is later sold to a real estate developer, who in 1971 demolishes it for a suburban tract.

■ Corona Avenue School, Bell, Los Angeles. The addition of a new wing to an older building. Glass walls of classrooms open to connected garden patios. The Ring Plan School without the ring. Widely published in education and architecture journals and featured on Hearst's Metronome News and "The March of Time" newsreel. Commonly called the "test tube school," it is compared by residents to "a drive-in market, an airplane hangar, and a penthouse on Mars."

1936

■ Plywood Model House, a small story-and-a-half structure, designed for an Architectural Building Material Exhibit, on Wilshire Boulevard, Los Angeles. Later moved to a wooded site in Westwood and acquired by architect Maynard Lyndon.

■ Kun house, Hollywood, Los Angeles. Entered from the top at street level via a modest garage and "gate house." The large, elegant two-and-a-half story villa beneath faces a steeply inclined ravine, with views of the city and ocean. The Kun House marks the debut of architectural photographer Julius Shulman after Neutra happens to see his superb snapshots of the house and henceforth encourages him to develop his talent.

1937

■ A banner year for Neutra as a number of significant buildings reach completion.

■ The Miller house, Palm Springs, California, an elegant synthesis of German modernism and Japanese refinement, with landscaping admirably adapted to the desert setting.

■ The Davis house, Bakersfield, California, with its cantilevered second-story balcony, a modernist homage to the nineteenth-century Monterrey Style.

■ The two-story Koblick duplex, Los Angeles, one apartment to each floor, tucked urbanely into a densely packed streetscape, with cantilevered balconies overlooking Silverlake.

■ The Darling house, San Francisco. Neutra's first redwood building, done in collaboration with his San Francisco associate Otto Winkler and with obvious references to the Bay Area tradition of William Wurster and Gardner Dailey.

■ The Hofmann house, Hillsborough, California, Neutra's first large Bay Area house in the high International Style.

■ The Ford house, San Francisco, Neutra's most interesting early effort at remodeling, with modernist renovations and front and rear additions to a Victorian San Francisco row house.

■ The Kraigher house, Brownsville, Texas, a sophisticated modern cottage for a bachelor airline executive. Neutra's first American building outside California.

■ The Catalina Ticket Office and Scholts Advertising Agency. Chic Los Angeles commercial buildings with minimalist, high-tech furnishing and accoutrements.

Sten house, Los Angeles, 1934.

Plywood Model House, Los Angeles, 1935-36.

■ The Landfair Apartments, Westwood, Los Angeles, which constitute Neutra's most urbane essay in the reciprocal imperatives of density and privacy. In essence a block of densely packed row houses, with staggered set-backs, unit by unit, augmenting the effect of separate, juxtaposed entities. The Landfair is in some respects an advance on the apartment buildings at the Weissenhofsiedlung (1927) by Mart Stam and J. J. P. Oud.

■ The Strathmore Apartments, Westwood, a modernist updating of two older regional traditions: the ancient, stacked megastructures of the Southwest Pueblo Indians and the more recent bungalow courts of Southern California. Strathmore contains six two-bedroom flats and two one-bedroom units, each with separate entrances to the terraced interior courtyard. Tenants include Luise Reiner, Orson Welles, John Entenza, and Charles and Ray Eames.

■ Neutra takes vacation to Mexico and visits painter Diego Rivera and architect Juan O'Gorman.

■ The magazine *Pencil Points* devotes its July issue to Neutra.

1938

■ A large house on the Santa Monica beach for MGM director Albert Lewin is entered via a long, elegant courtyard. The upstairs porch atop the curving bay of the living room recalls the Sten house. Both Lewin and the house serve as prototypes for a character and a house in Charles Reznikov's Hollywood novel, *The Manner Music*.

■ Designs a modernist version of the traditional San Francisco row house for William and Ilse Schiff, recent refugees from Nazi Germany. The street facade is a curtain wall of casements; the garden side an alternation of glass and stucco bands. Care is taken to defer on the interior to furniture the Schiffs have brought from Germany designed by Bauhaus graduate Harry Rosenthal.

■ A vacation house for John Nicholas Brown, Fishers Island, New York. Neutra's largest and grandest house outside California, it contains over thirty rooms to be staffed by six servants. Brown and Neutra incorporate Buckminster Fuller's all-metal prefabricated bathrooms. Painted with silver-gray aluminum paint, the sleek wooden house with its long bands of ribbon windows evokes the image of a train or ship and is given the name "Windshield." Heavily damaged by the unprecedented winds of the autumn hurricane of 1938. Rebuilt in 1939. Destroyed by fire in 1975.

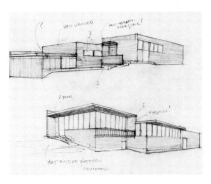

1939

■ McIntosh house, Los Angeles. Neutra's first redwood house in Southern California, built by clients who are willing to "go modern" at the insistence of their sons, who have learned of Neutra in art school. They are willing to venture into the brave new world of modernism, however, only if Neutra will forego the harder surfaces and materials of the International Style and build in the more familiar and "domestic" redwood.

■ Davey house, near Carmel, California. A large, elegant redwood house on the Monterrey peninsula that still uses the earlier abstract white stucco forms.

■ Sciobereti house, Berkeley, California. A small, crisp, two-story house for a University of California astronomer built of "cemesto" aggregate panels. Structurally and formally it relates to the Plywood Model House, Los Angeles (1936).

McIntosh house, Los Angeles, 1939.

■ Eurich house, Los Altos Hills, California. Built for a Stanford professor who had commissioned Neutra to design a house for him in Minneapolis when he was a professor at the University of Minnesota. Eurich's move to California confirms his desire to continue working with Neutra, who designs a house in the International Style — particularly effective in its skillful employment of low, screenlike exterior walls that extend the building into the landscape. The house has a lyrical informality that contrasts with Neutra's tauter style of the early thirties.

■ Becomes western region architectural consultant for the National Youth Administration (NYA) and builds functional and modestly handsome NYA training centers in Sacramento and San Luis Obispo, California. Serves as member and then chairman of the California State Planning Board from 1939 to 1941.

■ March: Arrival of third son, Raymond Richard Neutra.

1940

■ Beckstrand house, Palos Verdes, California. Neutra's first encounter with zoning codes that require pitched roofs. Here he takes advantage of the code's failure to specify the degree of pitch and makes the slant so minimal that the building reads from the ground as a typical Neutra flat-roofed modernist house.

■ Kahn house, San Francisco. Neutra's largest and best-known house in the Bay Area. Four stories tall, with an elevator leading to the top living room level. Perched high atop Telegraph Hill, the house has spectacular views of the city and the Bay. Flat roof, banded windows, cantilevered balconies, and white stucco with silver-gray trim identify the house with Neutra's sternest, purest style.

■ Avion Village, north of Dallas, Texas. Federally sponsored housing for defense workers, designed and planned in collaboration with Texas architects David Williams and Roscoe DeWitt. One- and two-story flat-roofed units grouped imaginatively along curving cul-de-sac streets in the "garden city" manner.

■ Evans Plywood Company Building, Lebanon, Oregon. Built of glass block and the company's own plywood, the orthogonal lines of the main volume of the building are pleasantly countered by a free-form, curving, two-story porch to the front and side. Above the first-floor offices are guest rooms used to house visiting company officials in the remote rural area.

1941

■ Works with Paul Williams, Welton Becket, Gordon Kaufman, and other Los Angeles firms in designing federally-sponsored Hacienda Village and Pueblo del Rio housing projects in southeast Los Angeles for predominantly poor black and Mexican-American populations.

■ Maxwell house, Brentwood, Los Angeles. A small wood and stucco house for two musicians. Neutra's first use of a pitched, gabled roof in straightforward deference to code restrictions and client wishes. In contrast to the modest and conventional street-front exterior, Neutra achieves dramatic interior effects by opening the living room ceiling to reflect the pitched roof, by glazing the gable to the ridge line, and by opening the room to a patio garden. House serves as a prototype for Neutra's Progressive Builders Homes (1942) for Burbank, California defense workers.

1942

■ Kelton Apartments, Westwood, Los Angeles. A modest but fetching triplex around the corner from Landfair and Strathmore. Two small, juxtaposed, ground-floor flats form the base of the larger, more lyrical "tree-house" apartment with inviting balcony roof decks stretching into the trees at front and back. Less tautly dramatic than Landfair and Strathmore, Kel-

Top: **Maxwell house, Los Angeles, 1941.**
Center: **Channel Heights Housing, Los Angeles, 1942.** *Bottom:* **Channel Heights Community Building, Los Angeles, 1942.**

12

ton looks ahead to Neutra's more informal work of the fifties.

■ Channel Heights Housing, a federally funded project for shipyard defense workers, near the Los Angeles harbor, San Pedro, California. The 222 residential structures provide housing for 600 families in one- and two-story, four-family units of shed roof design in stucco and redwood. Average cost per living unit is $2600. Most buildings face their streets at oblique 45-degree angles and offer their occupants views of the harbor and the ocean beyond. The finger-park, cul-de-sac planning provides a sense of both privacy and community. In addition to the residential units, Channel Heights offers a store and market building, a crafts center, a nursery school, and a community center.

■ Nesbitt house, Brentwood, Los Angeles. The nonindustrial materials reflect wartime shortages and client tastes, as well as Neutra's evolving style. A gently pitched shed roof rises from front to back and folds over the rear glass wall with a down-turning overhang. Board and batten redwood cover the exterior. Widely acknowledged as Neutra's masterwork of the early 1940s, the Nesbitt House wins a First Place award from the American Institute of Architects.

1943-44

■ Wartime moratorium on building.

■ Serves as visiting professor of design at Bennington College, Vermont.

■ Becomes chief planning and architectural consultant to government of Puerto Rico, developing prototype designs for medical and educational buildings to be constructed after end of wartime moratorium.

1944-45

■ Becomes wartime American-based president of CIAM. Represents the organization at various international conferences on postwar planning and reconstruction, including the San Francisco organizational meeting of the United Nations.

1946

■ Special Neutra issue of *L' Architecture D' Aujourd 'hui.*

■ Kaufmann house, Palm Springs, California, for Pittsburgh merchant Edgar Kaufmann, who ten years earlier had entered architectural history with his Fallingwater house by Frank Lloyd Wright. In the winter vacation California house, Neutra combines glass, stucco, natural rock, and silver-gray trim in a crisply elegant composition reminiscent of his great work of the 1930s. Sited on a 200 by 300-foot lot, with spectacular views of mountain and desert, the 3800-square-foot house forms a cross of two intersecting axes. Winner of an AIA Distinguished Award, the Kaufmann House will continue to be regarded as one of Neutra's greatest achievements.

1947

■ Norwalk Service Station, Bakersfield, California, becomes one of the first gas station designs by a major modern architect to be built. As published in architecture and in oil company journals, it has an especially wide influence on subsequent gas station typology.

■ Bailey Case Study House, Santa Monica Canyon, Los Angeles. The only realized building of the several that Neutra designs for John Entenza's *Arts and Architecture* Case Study program. A modest flat-roofed, redwood pavilion, enlarged in subsequent years with sympathetic additions designed by Neutra.

1948

■ Returns to Europe for lecture tour and reunion with relatives. First visit since 1930.

■ Tremaine house, Montecito, near Santa Barbara, California. A major transitional building in Neutra's style as it develops between the thirties and the fifties. The dominant material is natural stone with larger expanses of glass than ever before. A one-story cross-axial pinwheel plan with spaces flowing casually into one another.

Beautifully sited in a rolling foothill grove of giant live oaks and landscaped with rare succulent plants. Widely publicized and acclaimed, the house's warmer informality strikes an important nerve of a public obviously beginning to tire of the cool austerity of the International Style.

1949

■ First heart attack curtails activity and warns of greater problems to come.

■ Fame and recognition among laymen greatly enhanced by appearance on the cover of *Time* magazine. Cover story celebrates Neutra's leadership in the movement to "humanize" and "domesticate" the International Style.

1949-53

■ Joins architect-planner Robert Alexander in the planning and design of Elysian Park Heights, a massive low-income housing development for approximately 17,000 people in north-central Los Angeles's underpopulated Chavez Ravine. The use of high-rise towers to insure greater density arouses controversy in architecture and planning circles, but the project's death blow comes during the McCarthyite fifties from right-wing forces who see the development as "creeping socialism," if not rampant Communism, and the subversion of the values supposedly being defended at the time in the hills of Korea. Such groups as Citizens Against Socialist Housing (CASH), with the powerful backing of the *Los Angeles Times,* persuade the city council to reverse its earlier position of support and to jettison the ambitious project. Since the land has been cleared of most of its inhabitants, it lies empty throughout the fifties until the city makes it available for the vast Dodger Stadium when the Brooklyn team leaves New York and relocates in Los Angeles. Though their designs for Elysian Park come to naught, Neutra and Alexander's collaboration on it leads to a partnership in the 1950s.

13

1950

■ Northwestern Mutual Fire Association Building, Los Angeles, a well-proportioned and finely detailed commercial structure featuring the recently developed metal exterior louvers. Immaculate upkeep allows it to survive as a perfect fifties period piece. Neutra's last major public building that is designed before joining Alexander.

■ Publication of *Richard Neutra: Buildings and Projects, 1925-1950,* with introduction by Sigfried Giedion. First volume followed by subsequent ones in 1959 and 1966.

1951-52

■ Neutra & Alexander develop widely acclaimed plans for the redevelopment of downtown Sacramento and of the war-ravaged American island territory of Guam. Ultimate realization of both plans is disappointingly minimal.

■ Neutra's transition in the 1940s to warmer, more relaxed domestic architecture with greater use of wood and other "soft" materials, accented by the now-ubiquitous ornament of "spiderleg outrigging," reaches maturity in such commissions as the Logar and Hinds houses, Los Angeles; the Nelson house, Orinda, California; the Auerbacher lodge, Luring Pines, California; and the Moore house, Ojai, California. Neutra's favorite builder of his 1950s California houses is Fordyce "Red" Marsh. The new "California Modern" synthesis is also successfully conveyed to other areas and climates, as with the Fischer house, Spokane, Washington; the Everist house, Sioux City, Iowa; and the Price house, Bayport, Long Island, New York. All houses in this period are designed in Neutra's Silverlake studio, separate from the Neutra & Alexander office, which handles public and commercial structures.

1953

■ In addition to his developing flat-roofed modern style, Neutra continues to design convincing pitched-roof residences such as the neighboring and connected Hafley-Moore houses, Long Beach, California. His relationship with Alexander is strained, however, by the Silverlake office's design of such public and commercial structures as the San Bernardino Medical Clinic, a violation of the agreement that the smaller office would design only residences.

1954

■ Publication of *Survival Through Design,* Neutra's most important philosophic treatise, a collection of forty-seven short essays, a "loose, yet linked cycle of writings collected over a lifetime." The book's chief concern is architecture and the haptic sense, sensory stimuli and human responses, and the crucial relationships between the built environment and human psychological and physiological development.

1953-58

■ Neutra & Alexander's design for the National Charity League, Los Angeles (1953); Hacienda Motor Hotel, San Pedro, California (1954); Amalgamated Clothing Workers of American Building, Los Angeles (1956); and Arts and Sciences Building, St. John's College, Annapolis, Maryland, are sturdy, well-composed design accomplishments in the spirit of Neutra's pre-1950 work, though poor maintenance in each case sadly diminishes their once emphatic character. However, such later works as the Gettysburg Visitors Center, Gettysburg, Pennsylvania; the United States Embassy, Karachi, West Pakistan; and the County Hall of Records, Los Angeles, conceived before but completed after the breakup of the Neutra-Alexander partnership, display the cacophony of forms and materials that accompany the efforts of other modernists of Neutra's generation to "warm up" an architecture that is becoming stale and life-less. An exception to such problems of design and upkeep is Neutra & Alexander's Palos Verdes High School, a cluster of handsome white stucco pavilions with red-tile pitched roofs, overlooking the ocean.

1958

■ First one-man Neutra retrospective exhibition, at UCLA Art Gallery, Los Angeles.

■ Alexander informs Neutra that he finds it impossible to continue working with him, so great are the differences in their temperaments, principles, ideas, and working habits. Projects already begun will be completed, but no new commissions will be undertaken together.

1955-60

■ Despite the tension and problems in the Alexander office, Neutra's Silverlake office continues into the sixties to design successful and often brilliant houses in California and beyond. These include, among numerous others, the Perkins house, Pasadena, California (1955); the Chuey house, Los Angeles (1956); the Nash house, Camarillo, California (1957); and the Singleton house, Los Angeles (1959).

■ Neutra Archive established in 1955 at UCLA

1960

■ Publication of Esther McCoy's *Richard Neutra* in Braziller's "Masters of World Architecture" series.

1962

■ Publication of Neutra's autobiography, *Life and Shape.*

1960-66

■ After the closing of the Neutra & Alexander office, the Silverlake office of Neutra & Associates resumes the design of public and commercial commissions. Chief among these are the Bewobau housing developments near Hamburg and Frankfurt am Main, Germany, and the Garden Grove Community Drive-in Church, Garden Grove, California. The spectacularly sited Bucerius house, Navegna, Switzerland, typifies the office's growing number of European commissions.

1963-66

■ March 27, 1963: The Van der Leeuw Research House (1932) is almost completely destroyed by fire. It is redesigned by Neutra and his son Dion, a long-time associate in the various Neutra offices, with the basic gestalt and floor plan of the original house. But the rebuilt house (1966) reflects Dion's strong input in matters of detail, texture, color, and general ambience.

1966-69

■ Following the joint authorship of the Van der Leeuw Research House II, "Neutra & Associates" becomes "Richard and Dion Neutra." To give their son greater authority and independence, Richard and Dione live in Vienna, spending most of their time traveling on lecture tours. However, all work from the Los Angeles office is forwarded for the senior Neutra's approval and input. The Kemper house, Wuppertal, Germany (1967) and Delcourt house, Croix, France (1968), along with their American counterparts, bear an amazing resemblance in their blocky, horizontal configurations to the late work of Neutra's Dutch contemporary Gerrit Rietveld.

■ Neutra is interested, but perplexed, by Robert Venturi's *Complexity and Contradiction in Architecture* (1966) as he is by the dramatic late work of his own near-contemporary Louis Kahn, whose brooding, complex geometry runs counter to Neutra's modernist sensibilities.

1969

■ June: Neutra returns to Los Angeles to receive an honorary doctorate from UCLA, one of many such honors he receives in these years. He and Dione decide to re-sume residence at Silverlake.

1970

■ April: Neutra's unhappy restlessness demands the resumption of the peripatetic life, and he and Dione leave again for a European lecture tour. On April 16, a week after his seventy-eighth birthday, Neutra dies of a heart attack while visiting his own Kemper house, Wuppertal, Germany. Ashes returned to Los Angeles. Memorial service at Garden Grove church.

1977

■ Neutra is posthumously awarded the Gold Medal of the American Institute of Architects.

1982

■ Publication of first full-length biography and history of Neutra's work, by Thomas S. Hines.

■ 14 July, New York: Opening of Neutra retrospective at The Museum of Modern Art.

Neutra. Horse and serpent, 1915. Pencil, watercolor, gold paint.

Neutra. House in Trebinje, Serbia, 1915.
Pencil and watercolor on gray paper.

When five of Richard Neutra's buildings and projects were included in The Museum of Modern Art's "Modern Architecture International Exhibition" of 1932, Alfred Barr observed in his catalog preface that, "principally because of his writing" Neutra was "among American architects second only to Frank Lloyd Wright in his international reputation." But in fact by 1932 it was more than the two books on American architecture and the articles Neutra had published in 1931 that made him a consequential figure.

His work in California during the late twenties had won him worldwide professional acclaim. One building—the steel-framed Lovell house of 1927-29—became for a while indispensable to the iconology of modern architecture: it was an image of such persuasive authority that it seemed to promise whole chapters of revelation to come. In Europe by 1929 neither Gropius nor Breuer nor Mendelsohn had built houses of comparable sophistication. Mies had not yet built the Tugendhat or Berlin Exposition houses; Le Corbusier had completed several interesting houses but only one— the Stein house at Garches of 1927-28—that offered an architectural image of equal conviction and still greater sophistication.

Like Mies, Gropius, and Breuer after him, Neutra confirmed the American tradition of openness to new technology, from the Chicago balloon frame for wood construction to the steel frame for skyscrapers. The Lovell house was the first major work in the United States by an immigrant architect who, incidentally, had come here not because he was fleeing for his life but because he admired American energy and optimism, and wanted to understand better what they had already produced in order to add something of his own. Five years after his arrival he himself had become another distinctively American voice, heard with respect in the growing international community of architects. Yet the evolution of his work could not have been predicted from his

first exhilarating achievements, although in several respects it paralleled the evolution of modern architecture in general.

Immediately after World War II the expectations of the American middle class focused on the small suburban house (together with the indispensable automobile), and it was on the design of small houses that Neutra's practice, for better or worse, depended. By 1949 both the boom in house construction, especially in California, and Neutra's reputation were such that he could be featured on the cover of *Time* magazine (August 15) and described as "one of the world's best and most influential moderns"—ironically a judgment that by 1949 would no longer have been confirmed by his peers.

Vincent Scully, in his 1960 book on Frank Lloyd Wright, compared Wright's Fallingwater with the Lovell house ("both houses step forward over depressions"), noting Neutra's use of the "classic" steel frame construction that Wright had always abhorred, but avoiding any explicit suggestion that Neutra had in some way influenced Wright, his acknowledged master. By 1961 Scully was only slightly exaggerating the prevailing opinion when he omitted all buildings by Neutra from his book *Modern Architecture,* mentioning him once *en passant* as having been, with Mies, an architect "whose work was another synthesis between Wright and Europe."

Wright isolated himself in the Arizona desert when he was not on his Wisconsin farm, reviling at every opportunity developments in architecture he himself had helped set in motion. Neutra found a different kind of isolation: California. Virtually all his important work is in the southern part of that state. His clients and the kinds of commissions they brought him make up a social history of liberal, middle-class American aspirations as they worked themselves out during the Great Depression—but in the context of the one place in America where "dreams" were supposed to be lived. (It is a uniquely Californian pleasure to look from the Lovell house—a dream of health food and sunlit happiness sustained by labor-saving miracles of modern science—across a valley to Frank Lloyd Wright's Ennis house—a dream of dangerous ceremonies in the dark palace of a Mayan high priest—both buildings dependent on ingenious methods of construction and both beautiful monuments, now surrounded by cottage dreams in the less arduous Spanish mode.)

Neutra's dream, whatever it may have been, turned into a practice too often limited to houses for fifteen or ten or five thousand dollars for people who could scarcely afford them at any price. Rarely did he have a client whose resources were equal not simply to minimal requirements, but to providing him with a chance to expand and develop his ideas rather than repeat and reduce them.

After World War II, when modern architecture had begun to gain the patronage of business and government, Neutra's identification with the small house put him at a competitive disadvantage. His partnership with Robert Alexander from 1950 to 1960 brought larger and public commissions, and provided the personnel to handle them, but the resulting work bore too many of the characteristics of Neutra's small-scale design. Too often the office complexes and other work of the later fifties and sixties seems hasty, perfunctory, lacking any fundamental rethinking of possibilities.

In this failure Neutra was certainly not alone. The change from small to large scale, or from private to public, was not less problematic for Gropius and Breuer, among many others; it is a problem rooted in some of the fundamental assumptions of modern architecture perhaps even more than in the talents of its individual practitioners. Where many architects thought an exaggerated heaviness could give large buildings a more convincing presence, Neutra tended to increase the yardage, as it were, of his small-scale detail. The result is a repetitiveness moderated only by occasional "features" of dubious value. Younger architects, some of them trained by Neutra, and countless developers were already better at this kind of pastiche.

More successful, and certainly more interesting, were the changes that occurred in Neutra's house design. The Lovell, Beard, and von Sternberg houses, built from 1929 to 1935, were experiments with light steel construction, although nothing in the essentials of their conception precluded translating the same aesthetic to other materials and methods. That in fact was what Neutra did, more or less at the same time, in numerous other houses employing stucco or plywood on their closely spaced posts of wood or metal. But

Neutra, McIntosh house, Los Angeles, 1939.

By the mid-forties technical innovation and abstract stucco purity in the International Style are largely replaced in Neutra's work by two characteristic modes: a more extended and broken silhouette, occasionally with pitched roofs and contrasting walls of natural wood and white stucco; and a looser version of the structurally oriented aesthetic, as reworked in the Kaufmann house of 1946 and the Tremaine house of 1949. The latter in particular suggests, in its wide spacing of concrete piers, an awareness of the structural clarity and boldness that Mies van der Rohe's American work had begun to make so fascinating, although in fact Neutra had developed its structural design for Puerto Rican hospitals and schools, commissioned during the war but mostly unbuilt.

Neutra's work might have been expected to exert a wider influence on house design outside California than it actually did. When The Museum of Modern Art decided in 1949 to build a model house in its garden, Neutra was perhaps the obvious choice to design it. That he was not, and the reasons why, have some bearing on the development of architecture and criticism in the United States.

The American passion for something new in the way of model homes was rekindled by the Chicago World's Fair of 1933 and inflamed by the New York World's Fair of 1939. Chicago did better: its steel house by George Fred Keck was a successfully aggressive experiment in steel construction built too late to be included in Hitchcock and Johnson's "Modern Architecture" exhibition of 1932, for which it certainly would have been eligible. New York's Fair offered nothing of comparable interest, concentrating instead on historic styles made more "innovative" by appliance-laden kitchens.

In 1940 *Collier's* magazine sponsored a "House of Ideas" designed by Edward Stone and built in New York on a Rockefeller Center rooftop. Stone's reputation, which had already led to his collaboration with Philip L. Goodwin in designing The Museum of Modern Art, was based on several excellent houses in more or less International Style. But Stone too had begun to move away from his already relaxed version of its purity: *Collier's* house had a shed roof, and walls of unpainted boards, plywood, and shingles. It was, in *Architectural Forum's* double-edged comment, "an excellent example of a treatment which meets all of the common objections to the contemporary approach in residential

shortly before the war one client who disliked stucco requested redwood siding. Neutra obliged, and the McIntosh house of 1939 marked a new willingness to move toward an indigenous "tradition," later called the Bay Region style. It is rather less conspicuous in Los Angeles than around San Francisco but is not limited to Northern California, and the horizontal wood siding Neutra used in 1937 on the facade of a San Francisco townhouse had already shown that he could respond sympathetically to a context he found congenial. But the redwood board and batten Nesbitt house, begun in 1942 just weeks before wartime restrictions curtailed building, was the decisive integration of Neutra's personal idiosyncrasies with a regional idiom. The Nesbitt house was and still is a beautiful and even poetic building, and was immediately recognized as such.

Top: George Fred Keck. The Crystal House, 1934, Chicago World's Fair, 1933-34. *Bottom:* Edward D. Stone. Collier's House of Ideas, 1940, Rockefeller Center, New York City.

design." It would have seemed unnecessary to repeat that particular demonstration nine years later—at least not in a manner that so clearly acknowledged the force of the "common objections."

Frank Lloyd Wright's Usonian houses were too marked by such eccentricities as viewless kitchens—whatever their merits—to represent the kind of accommodation most Americans expected and the Museum wanted to emphasize as one of the advantages of modern architecture.

22

Neutra had just built the Bailey house, published by John Entenza in *Arts and Architecture* as one of a series of Case Study Houses begun by that magazine in 1945. It was an excellent one-story house, low and pavilion-like, and in itself it must have seemed a more plausible alternative to what Stone and Wright had been doing.

But the Museum was addressing a primarily regional audience, and wanted a building that would seem more at home in the New England climate. As an exhibition it would have to have a certain scale and presence, for which a delicate, one-story pavilion might have proved inadequate. The Museum also wanted to suggest some continuity between the ideas of the twenties and the beginning of the fifties, rather than suggest that for houses the International Style no longer seemed quite adequate even to those architects most closely associated with it. Neutra, in becoming more regional than international, had at the same time become almost as idiosyncratic as Wright.

Marcel Breuer and Walter Gropius had contended with these problems in the compact two- and three-story Gropius and Hagerty houses, among others, finding in flush vertical wood siding painted white a suitable New England equivalent to European stucco. Breuer had gone on to explore other treatments of wood siding in small houses that remained, in their use of walls as the surfaces of taut volumes, part of the international rather than the Wrightian version of modern architecture—and hence more related to what had been developing in public and commercial work.

These considerations ultimately made Breuer a convincing choice for the Museum's project. The house he built was surprising not for its use of unpainted wood siding but for its "butterfly" roof like an inverted gable. This configuration resembled the unbuilt house designed by Le Corbusier in 1930 for Mme Errazuriz, in Chile, and adapted in 1933 by Antonin Raymond for his own house built in Japan. Breuer's

Top: **Walter Gropius and Marcel Breuer. Hagerty house, Cohasset, Mass. 1939.** *Center:* **Marcel Breuer. House in the Garden, The Museum of Modern Art, New York, 1949.** *Bottom:* **Junzo Yoshimura. Japanese house in the Garden, The Museum of Modern Art, New York, 1954-55.**

version differed from these two predecessors in its internal spatial complexity, which was used not to make the living room more dramatic but to separate the master bedroom from other parts of the house by incorporating it under the two-story end of the roof. In its entirety the house was a lively illustration of a new kind of flexible planning more and more Americans were convinced they wanted. Its oddly pitched roof, besides yielding a memorable image, could also be explained as a friendly acknowledgment of tradition-bound neighbors, should there be any.

One other factor had influenced the Museum's choice. Breuer taught architecture at Harvard. Architects who wish to generate a professional following should teach, even if, like Wright, they have to do so in their own homes. Neutra had organized a short-lived course of lectures at a Los Angeles art school, but his role as teacher had been effectively limited to office apprentices. Among them were such distinguished talents as Harwell Harris, Gregory Ain, and Rafael Soriano, all of whom went on to do important work. (Largely on the strength of a row housing design much influenced by Neutra's Landfair and Strathmore apartments of 1937, Ain was asked to do a second Museum house in 1950. The Museum then wanted to show an alternative to the Levittown house; again Neutra was not considered suitable.) However, Neutra never had the continuing challenge of formulating a curriculum and being around long enough to see where students and teachers might take it.

Since news of his work could be had only from professional journals, Neutra became perhaps too energetic in pressing photographs of each new house on editors everywhere. The result was that even the interesting ones were published less often in the United States. In domestic architecture Breuer's influence was widely felt. The only strong alternative to his informal wood houses was the cool, elegant formality of Philip Johnson's brick-walled houses, adaptations of projects by Mies. Neutra's less imposing houses were, meanwhile, becoming at their best more delicate, more pavilion-like, and more recessive. To European editors his work was still a novel link between European finesse and American enterprise. By the mid-fifties the glass-walled office building had made finesse American, and European architects began to visit the United States to study such buildings and to work for their architects. Neutra's large-scale work was out of the running, and in any case California is a long way from New York or Chicago.

The third and final house built in the Museum's garden in 1954 was modeled on Japanese residences of the sixteenth and seventeenth centuries. Like Museum exhibitions on Indian Art of the United States (1941), or African Textiles and Decorative Arts (1972), it was intended to explain the parallels between modernism and the arts of other cultures. Japanese architecture had been acknowledged by Wright, Le Corbusier, and many others as a confirmation of their own ideas, if not as a direct source of inspiration. Neutra, like Wright, had a particular sympathy for Japanese design, evident in his work before he visited Japan in 1930 and wrote about what he had seen in two of his three articles for the German magazine *Die Form*. Much of the history of Neutra's architecture is illuminated by an examination of his own equivalents for selected items from the Japanese classical tradition, but before doing so it is instructive to consider certain aspects of his sensibility as a young artist.

23

Neutra. Farm building, Falkenberg, Germany, 1923. Charcoal.

Neutra. Self-portrait, 1917. Charcoal.

Neutra's talent far exceeded mere draftsmanship. Like Le Corbusier, he might well have pursued a separate career as an artist. Most of his early drawings are of value today for their pictorial qualities alone: their interest does not depend on any association with his architecture. Even the water-color studies of buildings made on his youthful travels and during World War I display a delicacy of color and value that makes their architectural content almost incidental. The dark landscapes in charcoal are painterly in their tonal masses, and might perhaps be seen today in the context of Chinese or Japanese painting if their intense melancholy did not recall the Vienna of Gustav Mahler. (China and Austria unite when one thinks of the orientalizing music, and Hans Bethge's translations of Tang dynasty poetry used as the text, of Mahler's "Das Lied von der Erde.")

The portrait drawings, notably those of his friend Meusser and of his wife's younger sister, Regula Niedermann, are sympathetic but detached, and specific in their details of character and deportment. Even a sleeping dog is sketched with the kind of unsentimental affection serious dog-lovers appreciate. Klimt and Schiele and perhaps Hodler are sometimes remembered, yet the best of these drawings suggest a personality already sure of itself even when, as in the later

Neutra. Landscape, 1918. Charcoal.

Neutra. Portrait of Hans von Meusser, 1918.
Charcoal.

Neutra. Portrait of Regula Niedermann,
1919. Pencil and pastel.

Neutra. Portrait of a woman, 1918. Pencil.

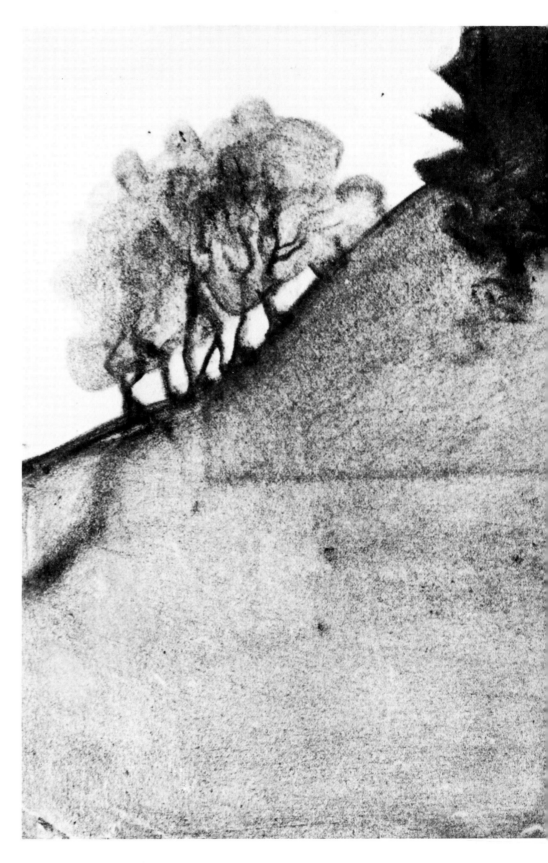

Neutra. Landscape, ca. 1918. Charcoal.

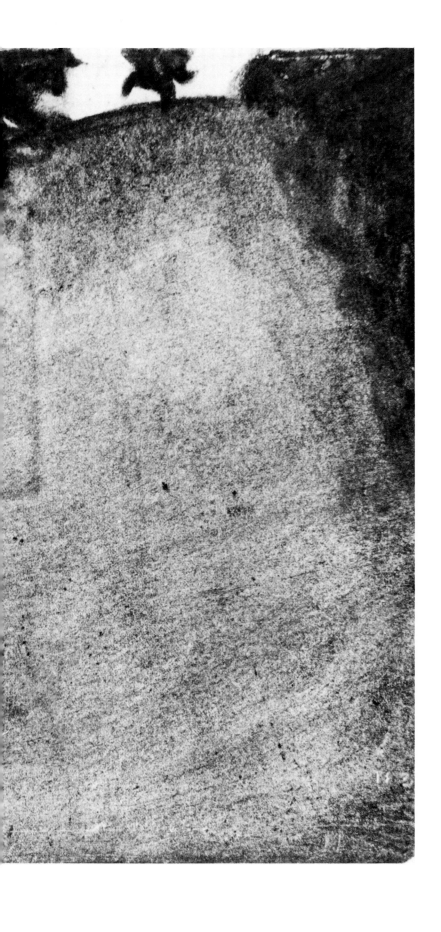

Neutra. "Fieber Nachtkatzen schreire,"
Feverish night cats stalking, 1918. Charcoal.

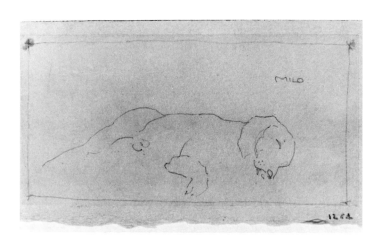

Neutra. *Milo,* ca. 1917. Pencil.

Neutra. Village crucifix, ca. 1915. Pencil and pastel.

Neutra. *Turkish Girls,* 1915. Pencil and watercolor.

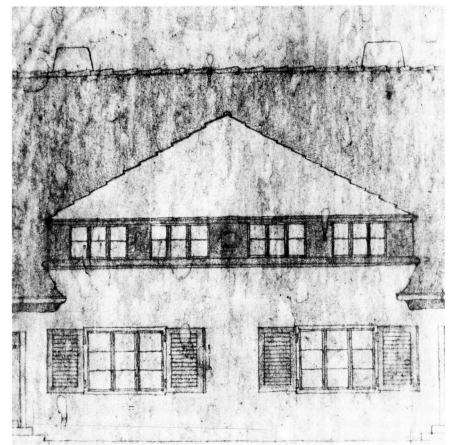

Neutra. Gatehouse? Forest Cemetery,
Luckenwalde, Germany (DDR),
1922 (project).

Top: Neutra. Unidentified buildings, Forest
Cemetery, Luckenwalde, Germany (DDR),
1922 (project). *Center:* Neutra for Erich
Mendelsohn. Berliner Tageblatt addition,
Berlin, 1922. *Bottom:* Neutra and
Mendelsohn. Zehlendorf houses, Berlin,
1923.

architectural drawings for Erich Mendelsohn, it deliberately explores the spirit of another man's work.

Only in an occasional picture like the watercolor of peasant girls—the kind of cheerful wartime souvenir one makes for parents and friends to show how colorful the natives look—does facility overcome observation. The result is a shift toward the style of the cartoonist, replacing authentic feeling with a predetermined method for capturing "effects." This facility was to undermine virtually all of Neutra's later drawings and ultimately affected the quality of his architecture.

Most of the pioneers of modern architecture made beautiful drawings of their buildings, especially in their younger days when clients were few and there was little to do except draw. Neutra was in some ways an exception. He did indeed make interesting architectural drawings, but they do not at first have anything like the force of his nonarchitectural work. Only later in the twenties does his vision rapidly come into focus with a style almost as personal as his handwriting.

Of the projects completed between 1921 and 1923, when he left for America, the housing and a municipal forest cemetery at Luckenwalde, Germany, are curious both for the childlike simplicity of their sketches and their traditionally Nordic architecture. The charcoal study for the corner addition to the Berliner Tageblatt building, done for Mendelsohn and presumably a variation on his design, is in the insistent horizontal manner of Mendelsohn's "modernistic" phase, as is the more interesting sketch for housing at Zehlendorf, Berlin, also done with Mendelsohn but for which he was publicly identified as the collaborating architect. Sketches for a library in Jerusalem recall the Wrightian origins of much European work, and it must have come as something of a shock to Neutra to be put to work by Wright, when he was invited to stay at Taliesin, not on one of the master's

Neutra. Library for the Jewish University, Jerusalem, 1923 (project).

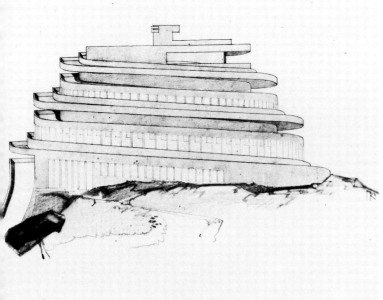

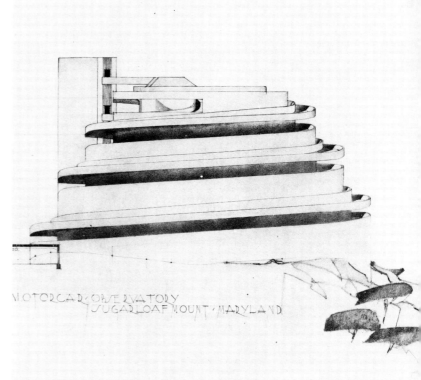

Neutra for Frank Lloyd Wright. Motorcar
Observatory, Sugarloaf Mountain,
Maryland, 1924 (project).

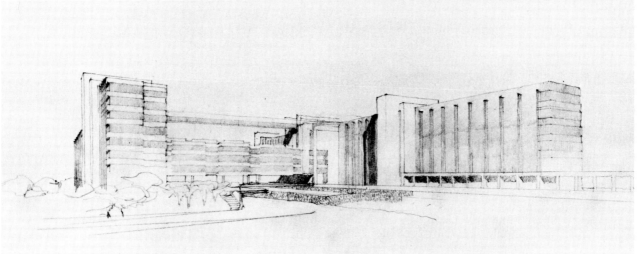

**Neutra and Rudolph Schindler. League
of Nations Building, Geneva, 1926
(competition project).** *Top:* lakefront.
Bottom: approach.

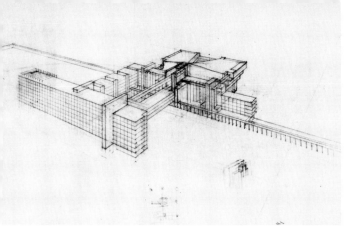

rectilinear, cross-axial designs but on a ziggurat for Sunday drivers. Neutra's perspective drawings for Wright's "motor-car observatory" or "automobile objective" are crisp, clear, and decorated with foliage in a manner obviously his own. He must have valued his work on this project; that he saved six drawings suggests he thought they were more than a record of his brief stay with Wright.

One of the best drawings done after settling in Los Angeles is for a 1926 League of Nations competition entry, designed in collaboration with his Viennese friend Rudolph Schindler, in whose house he lived and with whom he had formed an uneasy partnership. This handsome perspective is seen from the lake, in which four boats resembling trees in the drawings for Wright are placed like stepping stones to lead the eye toward the building's entrance. Another design of the late twenties also combines emphatically vertical and horizontal elements, in this case on adjacent walls of a skyscraper, anticipating the remarkably similar Philadelphia Savings Fund Society building by Howe and Lescaze.

Neutra's office building is one of several projects that were part of a prolonged urban design study called Rush City Reformed. Both as drawing and as architecture the image is skillfully composed. One interesting feature is the change in height in the middle of the long elevation, echoed in the corner shops. Another is the direct expression of structure in the corner cantilevers, not unlike Louis Kahn's Richards Medical Research Buildings of 1961-63. A variant tower design of the late twenties, for which there was supposed to be an actual client, carries Wrightian fin-like projections above the roof, while rounded corners and gleaming metal spandrels anticipate the Bowman Brothers apartment project of 1931 shown in the "Modern Architecture" exhibition the next year.

The combination here of forms and materials associated with industrial design, together with elements retrieved from Wright, foretells a development central to Neutra's individuality. Wright's "romantic" composition uses loosely composed, often asymmetrical design of intricate profile, mass, and surface, such calculated irregularity being particularly effective when deployed on a steep site. Neutra has been both praised and blamed for having cleaned up Wright's complications—a process with which he achieved significant results in the Lovell house of 1927-29.

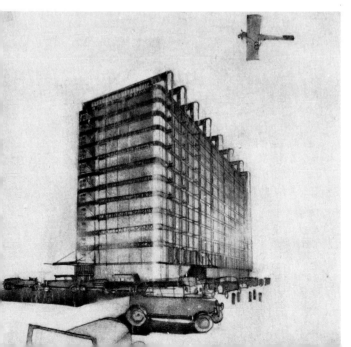

Top: **Aerial view of League of Nations Building.** *Center:* **Neutra. Office Building, Rush City Reformed, 1926-27.** *Bottom:* **Neutra. National Trading Center, ca. 1929 (project).**

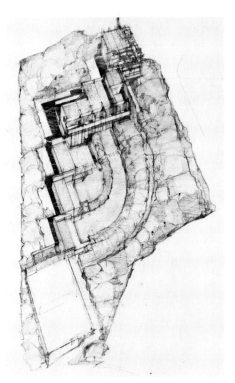

Neutra. Lovell house, first scheme,
ca. 1927. *Below:* Neutra. Lovell house,
second scheme, ca. 1927.

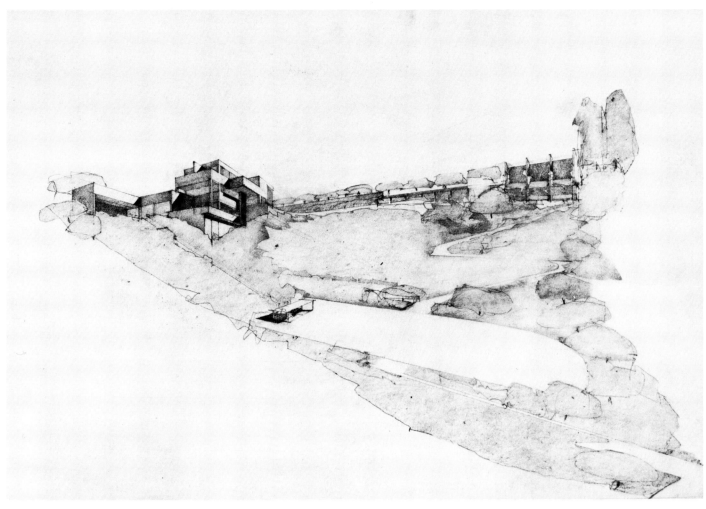

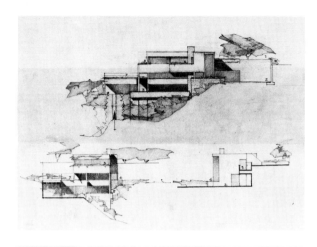

The Lovell house as built is at least the third version of the project. Of what appears to be the first version, only one drawing survives. It shows an L-shaped house stepping downhill in three levels from the roadside entrance at the top. Only two levels are clearly defined. Fin walls divide a long balcony at the third floor: lower walls appear to be glass. The offset masses are echoed in the stepped walls and earth ramps of the garden, which terminates at a tennis court. Dr. Lovell is associated with health regimens, yet nothing in this design suggests the elaborate exercise facilities eventually specified (but never completed) nor does the title yet bear the designation "Health House"—it is only a "Residence."

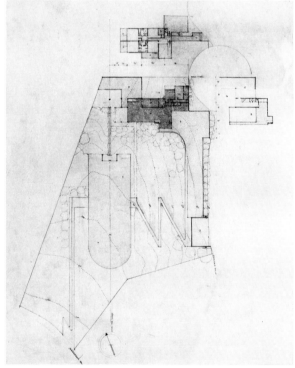

Three drawings survive for what seems to be the second version. An immediately obvious difference is that all levels are articulated: the elevations consist almost entirely of continuous parapets, some of them cantilevered as if pointing downhill. That part of the house along the road is smaller and the garage is now a separate building some distance to the south, connected to the house visually by a walled garden; there is no other architectural landscaping. The most interesting exterior feature is a two-story roofed terrace, and besides the narrow glazed stairwell opening into the living room there is one other indication of internal volumetric development. The perimeter configuration differs on each floor but not so much that the sense of a single volume is lost. The structure shows no evidence of modular equalization and there is no expression of steel, but the disposition of rooms on the plan is close to the final version.

Ten exterior perspectives and elevations of the house, five of the garage, five interior perspectives, and all the working drawings survive to illustrate the development of the third scheme. A visible structural module now makes its appearance, stressed as thin vertical lines that provide a steady rhythm in contrast to horizontal bands of irregular length and

Neutra. Lovell house, second scheme, ca. 1927. *Top:* elevation. *Center:* plan. *Bottom:* Neutra. Lovell house, final design, 1929: steel frame in construction.

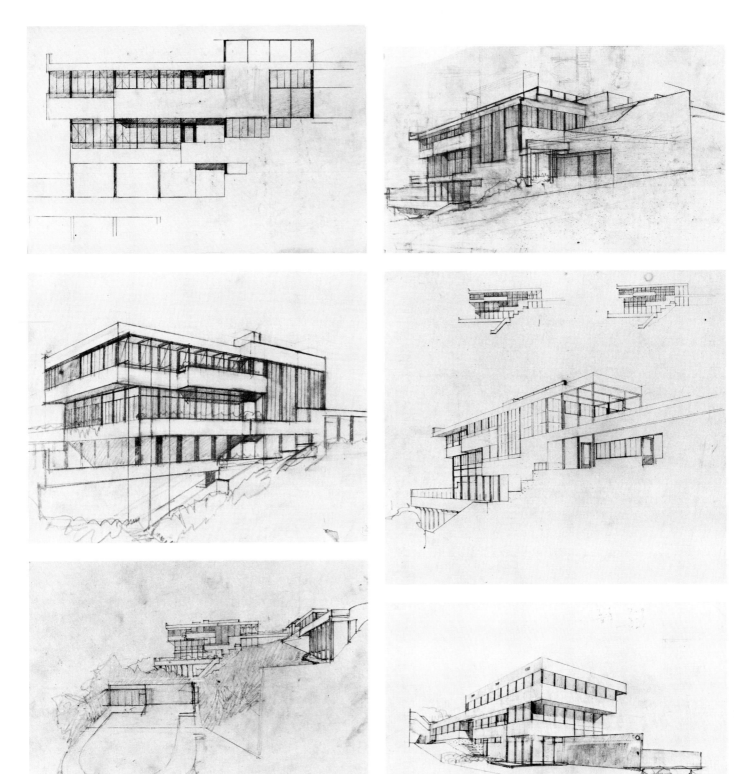

height. Neutra was understandably proud of his enterprising use of open-web joists (then new) and four-inch-square steel posts spaced at intervals of five feet two inches on center and fitted with standard steel casement windows. His handling of these elements exploits some of the ambiguities of steel construction, so that what appear to be cantilevers are actually suspended from the roof with the same "supporting" posts. What he did not discuss—perhaps because he thought it would seem unscientific—was the grouping of horizontal bands of metal lath sprayed with white stucco that make up the parapets.

These bands, already present in the second scheme, are now broken and pulled apart. The bottom-most extends furthest out, forming part of a base that contains a swimming pool. At the opposite end of the elevation two more horizontal bands extend away from the house, one of them connecting to the garden wall, the other enlarging the apparent volume by forming a kind of frame in space that suggests a pergola. Another band at the base drops diagonally to connect with the sloping site, and above it two bands at different heights come together in a patch of wall. Not all these bands are on the same plane: the parapets, and the steel structure with and without its windows and screens, separate and meet again. At the stairwell the steel grid breaks through the banding altogether.

Neutra. Lovell house, 1928.
Opposite page: **preliminary studies.**
Below: **final design.**

LOVELL HOUSE

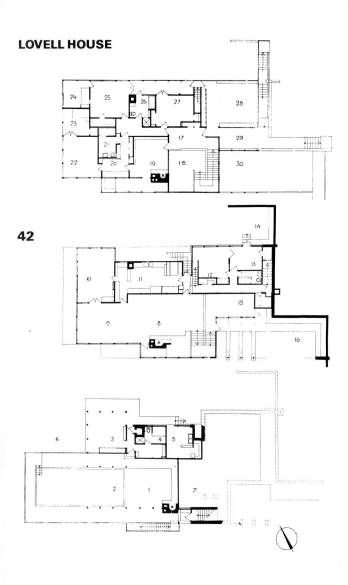

1 Playground
2 Swimming pool
3 Nursery porch
4 Shower
5 Laundry
6 Gym court
7 Unexcavated
8 Living room
9 Dining room
10 Porch
11 Kitchen
12 Guest room
13 Guest room
14 Patio
15 Library
16 Patio
17 Entry
18 Stairwell
19 Study
20 Dressing room
21 Bath
22 Living room
23 Sleeping porch
24 Sleeping porch
25 Living room
26 Bath
27 Living room
28 Terrace
29 Entrance terrace
30 Patio below

From its top-floor entrance the house appears only one story high, although there are views from the entrance terrace to the garden below. Bedrooms are at the top; one level down are guest rooms, kitchen, and a four-part living area with access to the garden; the bottommost level contains the swimming pool and utilities. Virtually the entire perimeter consists of steel window frames either glazed or screened. Each bedroom suite comprises a "living room" opening on to a screened sleeping porch, and a screened porch was also provided next to the dining room.

The best-known photograph of the house (*opposite bottom*) was taken before the glass and the screens were installed and consequently emphasizes the web-like structure and the internal volumes, the latter subsequently obscured by curtains.

The entrance hall (*top left*) overlooks the large, bright stairwell; through the open door is Dr. Lovell's study. The two-story seating area with fireplace was intended as the main living room. From it one looks toward what was the original dining room. This was subsequently transferred to an adjacent porch, thus extending the living area. The library (*top right*) is part of the living room suite and opens directly onto the garden.

The circular fixtures mounted on the stair wall are made of Ford headlights. Glossy paint and wood panelling, suspended metal light troughs, and pale gray carpet contribute to the look of austere industrial modernism.

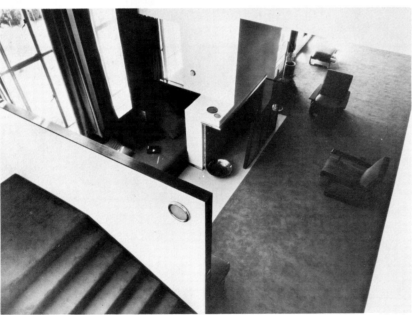

48

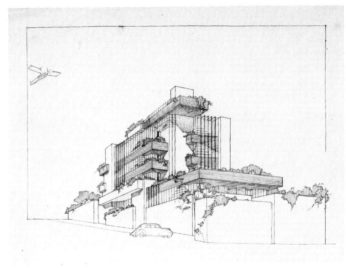

No single element determines the composition. The point of the design is that each element is subject to inconsistent variation, or what might now be seen as a methodical kind of "complexity and contradiction." If there is a fault it is that one element is allowed to dominate the rear (northern) elevation, and not that one of the horizontal bands is steel painted gray rather than white stucco. In two of the elevation studies this band and the glass are toned gray, as if in shadow. Neutra evidently decided to build the shadow permanently into place, to reinforce the staccato rhythms of the interrupted banding, and also to echo the uninterrupted verticality of the stairwell. It is a beautiful and subtle weaving of line and plane, intuitively balanced and, for all its intricacy, serene. The house seems to be walking, or floating, as Neutra liked to describe it, out of the site. The image was compelling: Rudolph Schindler's Oliver house of 1933 restates Neutra's composition, miniaturizing it in a design whose relation to Cubism removes it still more from Wright, who seems to have had a characteristic response of his own.

Working drawings for the Lovell house were made by Neutra himself and are dated "April 6, 1928," or "June '28" for several sheets of steel details. The final design appears to have been completed during 1927 or, at the latest, the first three months of 1928. Wright's 1929 apartment project in Los Angeles for Elizabeth Noble invites comparison with the Lovell house for its different treatment of similar elements, particularly the glass walls interwoven with parapets, although Wright's genius and the richness of his invention were so protean that the Noble project is explicable without

Top left: **Neutra. Lovell house, 1929.**
Top right: **Schindler. Oliver house, 1933.**
Bottom left: **Neutra. Lovell house, 1928.**
Bottom right: **Frank Lloyd Wright. Noble apartment house, Los Angeles, 1929.**

reference to Neutra. Nevertheless, it is a curious coincidence that in both the Noble apartment house and the project for an apartment tower on New York's St. Mark's in the Bowerie, also of 1929, Wright should have pursued the combination of a light metal grid interwoven with solid bands. In Wright's usage the grid is clearly nonstructural; cantilevers make it difficult to tell how the parapets are supported; and the composition is characteristically both more dynamic and more three-dimensional.

Both the Noble apartment building and the Lovell house are in different ways implicit in some of Wright's much earlier buildings, perhaps most notably the 1917 Odawara country hotel project in Nagoya, Japan, which was to have occupied a site similar to that of the Lovell house. Of the Noble apartment house Henry-Russell Hitchcock observed, in his 1942 monograph on Wright, that "its bold contrast of plain concrete surfaces and large open glass areas...parallels remarkably closely the principles, supposedly so antithetical, of the 'international' architects of Europe."

In Europe Rietveld and Mies translated the Wrightian picturesque into the language of abstract painting. Their architecture advanced by selectively simplifying some of Wright's ideas. Neutra's architecture advanced by a method intuited less from abstract painting, which seems to have left him unmoved, than from the Japanese sources he and Wright both admired. With the Lovell house Neutra arrived at his own version of what has been called Romantic Rationalism, which is to say that he found a simple way to be complicated. His principal instrument of design, however, is neither the structure nor the ribbon window; it is the horizontally extended solid parapet, borrowed in the first instance directly from Wright, and for which Wright's Gale house of 1909 is among the "purest" of early examples.

Neutra deserves some credit for having confronted Wright with a transformation of his own ideas that was difficult to ignore, an achievement that distinguished him from so many of Wright's disciples. But Wright may well have felt he could do it better. "Cheap and thin" was his characterization of Neutra's work, repeated to Hitchcock and Philip Johnson in 1932 until it elicited Hitchcock's written reply: "We are forced to interpret your opposition to this man who has frequently expressed his indebtedness to you as due to a jealousy at once meaningless and undignified."

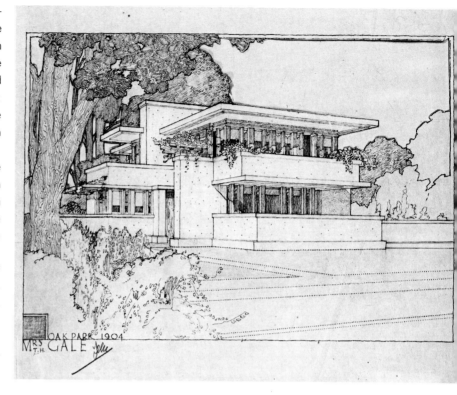

Frank Lloyd Wright. Gale house, Oak Park, Illinois, 1909 (drawing 1904).

Although during the thirties his architecture moved further toward a more compact kind of composition, the Lovell house contained most of the ingredients Neutra later reworked. They are the parapet or spandrel; the ribbon window; the overhanging roof; the thin wall plane; and the steel or wood skeleton structure.

These discrete elements are sometimes made to interact in surprising ways. On the Lovell house, for example, the "flat" roof actually has a considerable pitch toward the south. This allowed the southern elevation to be capped by a thinner horizontal band than those made by the parapets. But on the western elevation the full parapet dimension is restored, making a jog at the corner that terminates the southern elevation with a kind of exclamation point. The same device is used on the west windows of the bedroom floor just below, where it has no practical origin, and it also became one of Neutra's favorite means of enlivening the interior space of small rooms.

The parapet or spandrel has another use that is almost as important: its extension away from the building to define an outdoor area by means of an overhead frame. Wright characteristically attached his houses to the landscape by low, ground-hugging garden walls. In a sense Neutra lifted these up into the air, but his use of such wall elements to describe a space is perhaps more conditioned by interior design. The use of a narrow band of white plaster above wood panelling of course goes back to the Elizabethans, and was adapted by Wright as well as by the Europeans. (Mies's Riehl house dining room can stand for dozens of examples.) In Japanese architecture the strip of plaster wall, called *kokabe,* above the sliding doors became a principal means, especially in the way it was related to the ceiling plane, of unifying a room whose elevations might all be different. In some Japanese usages these overhead bands might be of different heights, their intersections calling attention to a feature such as a

Top: **Ludwig Mies van der Rohe. Riehl house, Berlin, 1907.** *Top center:* **Guesthall, Saikyo-ji Temple, Japan. 1598.** *Bottom center:* **Neutra. Landfair Apartments, Los Angeles, 1937.** *Bottom:* **Neutra. Hofmann house, Hillsborough, Cal., 1937.**

corner alcove. Neutra turned this upside down, using such jogs for changing windowsill heights so that attention is directed toward the floor plane rather than the ceiling. But just below the ceiling he often retained a much narrower band of white plaster (its Japanese equivalent is called *arikabe*), apparently being more concerned to reinforce the perimeter of a room than to let the space flow out through the windows by way of an uninterrupted ceiling plane. And quite often he develops the lower wall as a dark, sometimes shiny, wood surface that also recalls Japanese precedent.

Steel casement windows ostensibly ordered out of a catalog are at first used by Neutra as if they had to be repeated *ad infinitum*. In the Lovell house the elevations use virtually continuous windows of identical width, only their height being varied on some elevations by the addition of a third light at the bottom. The reason for such uniformity, apart from the alleged practicality of the windows, is the desire to maintain the closely spaced perimeter rhythm of the steel structure, which if repeated enough takes on the character of a woven fabric. In this Neutra's earlier work relates to the delicate structure of Japanese tea house and garden architecture rather than to the bolder, more formal post and lintel style of temples and mansions. A detail from the gardens of Katsura Palace makes the point: the wall plane is preserved by closely spaced vertical members analogous to the steel frames of Neutra's casement windows. And his feeling for what is architecturally essential was heralded as early as 1915 by his first work: an Officers' Tea House of slender post and lintel construction, like a Turkish kiosk with a flat roof.

Whatever analogies may be made with Japanese design, one difference is striking. For Neutra the module is a useful device for organizing the rhythm of the *wall:* it is not a true plan module like a tatami, because it only indirectly influences the proportions of rooms. Instead it leads to an undifferentiated perimeter rhythm made up of redundant structure. In later years Neutra began to use large sheets of fixed glass and finally eliminated his narrow window module—by then a Neutra trademark—in favor of structural elements more widely spaced and boldly defined.

Smooth white surfaces were considered a necessary, or at least desirable, qualification for a style that aspired to the universal aesthetic of the machine age. In photographs, especially those taken in the twenties and thirties, the

Top: **Katsura Villa, Kyoto, 17th century, side entrance to veranda.**
Bottom: **Neutra . Officers' Tea House, Trebinje, Serbia, 1915.**

Neutra. Koblick house, Los Angeles, 1938.

method too cumbersome for other, smaller buildings, Neutra never used it again.

Minor technical problems marred Neutra's buildings as they did those of many other architects in the same period. In the Lovell house it is essential to the conception that the roof be simply another white band. But in later work Neutra often sheathed the roof fascia in metal, which like the windows and the columns, was painted a silver-gray meant to suggest "industrial" production. Metallic paint soon faded and lost any sheen it may have had, and the drab effect was often made more tawdry by sheet metal that buckled and split. This lack of attention to facts about the behavior of materials is inexplicable when, at the same time, Neutra was able to refine inexpensive steel construction methods whose details he most certainly mastered.

Early in the thirties Neutra began to replace a visible roof cap at the top of the fascia with a thin projection at the bottom. It functions as a gutter and sometimes extends well beyond the corner of the roof—a compelling but fragile detail not unrelated to some of the linear extensions of structure in Gerrit Rietveld's 1923 Schröder house, and other de Stijl designs. By the fifties this kind of schematic linear extension is done with a beam projecting several feet beyond the roof it carries, to terminate at a thin supporting post. Their very flimsiness no doubt made such details inexpensive and appealing, especially when combined with nearly invisible butt-jointed glass corners. These are not simply Wrightian "open" corners. A real structural corner is emphasized, but it is placed just outside the room. The separation quite noticeably enlarges interior space. Ultimately the detail of the corner "outrigger" becomes predictable and even obsessive, yet in certain cases it is effective beyond all reasonable expectations.

Two other interior details play a great part in Neutra's design. Long, low storage cabinets just below the windows reinforce a sense of enclosure (and when combined with a desk recall their origin in the Japanese *shoin* [desk] furniture customarily placed before a window); and mirrors at the end of a wall prolong the window rhythm while doubling the view. Mirrors and modernism do not combine easily. To purists mirrors belong among the dubious theatrical properties of the interior decorator. Adolf Loos, for a short time Neutra's mentor in Vienna, had used them lavishly in some of his commercial work; even Le Corbusier had flirted

stucco walls do indeed look smooth and the buildings were still too new to show cracks and stains. Sparkling in the California sun, most of Neutra's early stucco houses are in this respect more convincing emblems of the International Style than Europe could offer. Photographed from a distance the Lovell house looks as trim and precise as its abstract composition requires, but in reality its stucco surfaces are rough, lumpy, and soft at the edges. So far from suggesting industrial precision, they recall the uncertain skills of an arts-and-crafts class making its first clay pot. This was the result of spraying the stucco on, rather than trowelling it, and whether because he did not like the effect or found the

Top: Neutra. Singleton house, Los Angeles, 1959. *Bottom right:* Neutra. Nash house, Camarillo, Cal., 1957. *Bottom left:* Neutra. Price house, Bayport, L.I., New York, 1953.

with mirrors (in the library of the Church house, 1928) before renouncing them for more substantial indulgences. But Netura seems never to have lost his taste for illusion as a harmless and amusing way to alter the confines of a room.

All these details of design have been enumerated without regard to the plan—which for modern architecture is supposed to be, along with structure, the decisive factor. Of course it need not be, and Neutra's planning is remarkable for its undogmatic, perfectly straightforward dealing with his clients' preferences. Neutra made much of getting to know his clients, subjecting them to long interviews and detailed questionnaires. The latter must often have kept them busy for at least the few days he needed to design a house. In any case there is no reason to doubt his sympathetic curiosity about his clients' lives. What is striking, however, is the similarity of the solutions to what each of them may have believed were uniquely personal requirements.

Neutra's plans are readily characterized: for narrow city lots a T shape, the stem being used for the living room, the rest for garage, kitchen and bedrooms, sometimes with a second floor over this part alone; for less confined sites other standard designs are L-plans, pinwheels, and long rectangles whose elevations are interrupted by occasional jogs. But never in his American work does he encompass all the rooms of a one- or two-story house in a simple, unbroken rectangular box.

Where Breuer and others were concerned to prevent the "public" living room volume from being overwhelmed by the larger "private" bedroom volume, Neutra sidestepped the problem quite deftly by careful placing of the living room. All of his layouts are distinguished by tight management of room sizes, partitions, and closets, which gives the plans a greater intricacy on paper than they have in reality.

After the Lovell house only the house for Josef von Sternberg boasts a double-height interior space. Either such volumetric exercises did not interest Neutra, or his clients could not afford them; the former was most likely the case. More surprising is that he was not interested in anchoring a living space so that it seems less like a corridor or a hotel lobby; this is particularly problematic in such pinwheel plans as the Kaufmann and Tremaine houses. Unlike Wright, Neutra seems not to have felt any need for sheltering, cave-like corners. Entrances too are perfunctory; in some of the smaller houses the front door is in the corner of the living

Top: **Neutra. Neutra (VDL Research) house, Los Angeles, 1932. Patio.**
Bottom: **Raphael Soriano. Case Study House, Los Angeles, Cal., 1950.**

room, sometimes shielded by a low cabinet. No doubt such casual arrangements reflect owners' habits in using garage-to-kitchen access, but these vestigial entrances destroy psychologically much of the space they are meant to save. This defect is scarcely inherent in Neutra's aesthetic, and there are notable exceptions even among the smaller houses.

Some of Neutra's houses are so small that they can be correctly described as efficiency apartments (the American euphemism for *existenz minimum*) and his assortment of design details is often just right for their miniature scale. Nothing in their appearance suggests that they are, most of them, so small because they are so inexpensive. That is no negligible achievement. At the same time it must be said that having arrived at highly refined plans, after the fifties the Neutra office was content to repeat them without further thought.

And it is strange that his own house on Silverlake Boulevard and the house for Josef von Sternberg contain his only examples of completely enclosed patios. Everywhere else his architecture is unreservedly extroverted—admittedly toward interesting views. The Neutra house has such a view, but its richly planted private patio introduces a welcome alternative. The von Sternberg house, on the other hand, had a large and architecturally bold walled patio without any planting at all (pg.66). On published plans Neutra tended to use the label "patio" for virtually any outdoor sitting area no matter how unsheltered. Perhaps the notion of a house even partly turned in on itself reminded his clients too much of California's "traditional" Spanish Colonial houses. Whatever the reason, it was a neglected possibility that could have done much to widen Neutra's range.

This relationship between inside and outside is somehow problematic in Neutra's architecture. Glass is used abundantly and is almost always shielded by overhanging roofs. Rooms are clearly defined and the obvious attempts to merge indoors and outdoors are carefully limited. One moves easily from room to garden. The sense of physical well-being they produce is one of the most persuasive aspects of modern architecture in its California Style, as such living arrangements came to be called in popular magazines. Yet it is possible to sit in a Neutra living room and wish that one could get indoors. Whether there is too much sunlight is a subjective judgment, perhaps, and given the

California climate and the usual dramatic view it might seem perverse not to open a house to the outside. "Survival Through Design" was the title Neutra gave his collection of essays on the relation of architecture to human physiology, and the necessity, as he had come to think, of designing for the full range of nonvisual pleasures. In practice this benevolent concern may not always have succeeded. And nature abuses its champions as well as its despoilers. "Here you can grow trees in a desk drawer," John Entenza used to tell visitors to Los Angeles, and the beautiful gardens Neutra designed have often grown to conceal his buildings.

What is it, then, that makes so many of Neutra's houses so pleasant to be in? In one sense they have the virtues of their defects: the smaller they are the more agreeable their amenities. Neutra's architecture can be experienced as a collection of details. The purpose of any underlying conceptual theme of structure or space such buildings may have is to allow for a pleasing distribution of details. As a result the architectural ensemble is psychologically manageable because its components are small, varied, and can be taken one at a time. Nothing overwhelms. There are no stupendous architectural effects: every important design decision is

Charles Eames. Eames house, Santa Monica, Cal., 1949.

made in response to what is outside. For all their neatness Neutra's houses often give the impression of having been designed "freehand"—they suggest spontaneity and improvisation. The atmosphere created is calm but enlivening, and invariably they have a cheerful aspect difficult to define but evidently quite desirable to new owners who are now refurbishing some of them. It is that same well-meaning subordination to the natural scene that also makes its contribution to extrovert architecture. In a Neutra house there is no place to be sad.

If his work can be said to have had architectural progeny they are recognizable more by their structural themes than by any other aspect.

Neutra's experiments with load-bearing walls made of steel channels (Beard and von Sternberg houses) were soon abandoned and have had no successors, although Frank Lloyd Wright's 1937 sketches for California hillside houses, using the same material, are even thinner in the handling of wall and roof planes: Wright proposed a two-inch-deep channel to make walls and cantilevered roofs so thin their ends can be read as single lines. Prefabricated wall frames containing windows, like those Neutra used for the Beckstrand house, suggest a far more efficient use of steel, but among California architects Raphael Soriano, Craig Elwood, and Pierre Koenig have all preferred less redundant structural systems.

The most persuasive development of a Neutra theme was the work of Charles and Ray Eames in 1949 for their own Santa Monica house. Like Neutra's Bailey house just down the road, it was a Case Study for the magazine *Arts and Architecture*. Again steel posts, windows, joists, and doors are combined, but this time in a two-story volume that emphasizes horizontals only moderately and owes nothing else to Wright. And yet, in its asymmetrical play of glass and colored stucco panels filling a shoji-like grid, it looks even more Japanese than do the conventional pitched-roof developers' houses in various Pacific-region styles. Like so many of Neutra's works, the Eames's house is another much-admired "prototype" no one has seen fit to develop.

Neutra's success with small buildings outweighs his problematic results with larger compositions. He was an artist of the keyboard rather than the orchestra: he wrote *ballades*, not symphonies. His first achievement was to "rationalize" the irrational, and in this his efforts were assisted by the

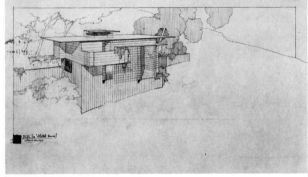

propaganda of the International Style. His second achievement was to transform his faith in technological modernity into something more substantial. But if his intuitively free style changed in response to realities, rather than to the advantages of an anticipated industrialization, it remained a style fundamentally committed to modern architecture. When he looked back to the wide-ranging idioms of the Bay Region, it was without the consciously historicising intentions that now motivate the post-moderns.

Neutra is most at home among those American artists for whom abstract form is the necessary way of dealing with metaphysical questions; but the questions somehow find their most cogent symbols in the natural landscape rather than in the forms of art. For Neutra as for Wright, landscape was more important than history. But because Neutra's buildings are never organically inextricable from their sites, their urbane forms divert attention from his essentially anti-urban, anti-technological sensibility. Beneath his professional optimism was an intelligence more thoughtful, more private, more hesitant, than the certainties of the twenties allowed.

Top: **Neutra. Beckstrand house, Palos Verdes, Cal., 1940. Prefabricated steel wall frames.** *Bottom:* **Frank Lloyd Wright. "All Steel" house, Los Angeles, 1937 (project).**

NEUTRA HOUSE

Called the VDL Research House in honor of C. H. Van der Leeuw, the Dutch industrialist who helped finance it, Neutra's home and office resolves a complicated program with seemingly effortless elegance. The house consists of a two-story wing fronting Silverlake Reservoir, connected by a service core to a one-story wing at the rear. Living quarters are on the second floor overlooking the lake; Neutra's offices are on the floor below. A patio and garden room are served by a second kitchen, and there is also a game room and a miniscule "bachelor's apartment." The lake elevation is lightened by the extra height of its upper windows and the thin overhanging roof, as well as by a recessed terrace. It is one of Neutra's most livable plans, modified by preferences perhaps more European than American, including the private patio.

The twilight photographs shown here were made by Luckhardt in 1932; in more conventional sunlit views taken later landscaping obscures the house. Destroyed by fire in 1963, it was subsequently rebuilt in modified form by Neutra and Dion Neutra, his son and architectural associate.

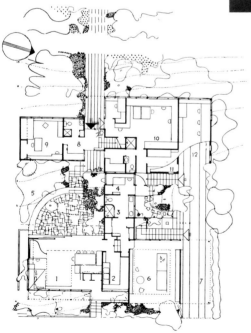

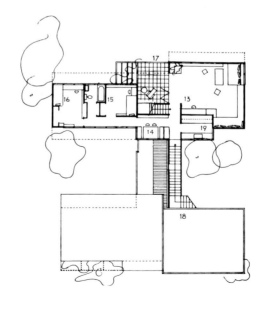

Ground Floor Plan

1 Living and recreation
2 Kitchen
3 Bathroom
4 Bedroom
5 Patio
6 Playroom
7 Car drive
8 Lobby
9 Studio
10 Office
11 Workroom
12 Garage below

Second Floor Plan

13 Living room
14 Dining area
15 Bedroom
16 Bedroom
17 Terrace
18 Roof
19 Kitchen

NEUTRA HOUSE

The second-floor terrace is separated from the living room by folding glass doors. Roof soffits contain screened openings for ventilation and continuous strips of recessed lighting.

BEARD HOUSE, ALTADENA, 1934

Neutra's second experiment in steel construction was the house for William Beard, son of the historians Charles and Mary Beard. Steel channels intended for floor construction were used to make load-bearing hollow walls; a cement floor rests on open-web beams and the roof is carried on open-web joists. The steel shell thus forms a plenum around the interior surfaces, and warm air circulated through it provides radiant heating. In summer, low openings in the outer wall admit air cooled by water sprinkled on adjacent bushes. The system is efficient but presents maintenance problems.

Exceptionally delicate framing details for the sliding glass walls in the living room are in scale with the module of the exterior walls, as is the open stair to the roof of the bedroom wing (intended to accommodate an additional two bedrooms). The entire building was painted glossy silver gray, which contributed to the look of an industrial artifact set down in startling contrast with the lush California landscape. Today Neutra's "high tech" finishes are easier to produce and maintain.

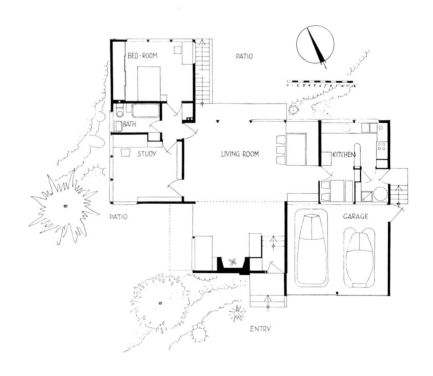

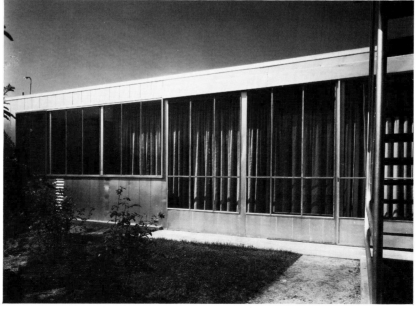

BEARD HOUSE

The corner of the living room (*above*) in which Neutra is standing is shown before installation of a dining table and built-in seats; the area is demarcated by the higher windowsill.

VON STERNBERG HOUSE, SAN FERNANDO VALLEY, 1935

With flag flying and palisades glistening in the sun, the well-known film director's house looked like an army outpost. Its steel walls coated with aluminum paint resembled those of the Beard house, but a moat surrounding the walled patio (left unplanted) and a two-story living room made it unusually luxurious. Occupied for a time by the novelist Ayn Rand, the property was acquired by a developer who demolished the house overnight.

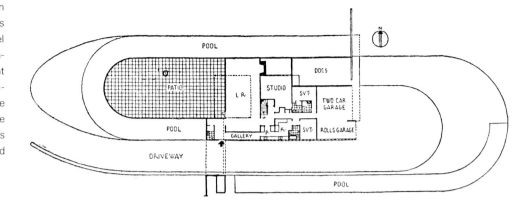

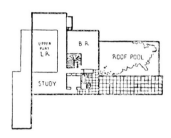

Interior views show the house before it was furnished by von Sternberg; photo at bottom right shows the living room as furnished by Ayn Rand.

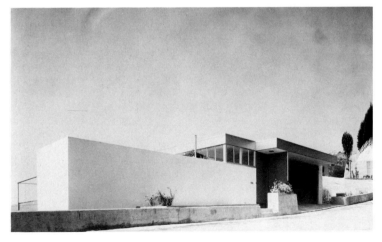

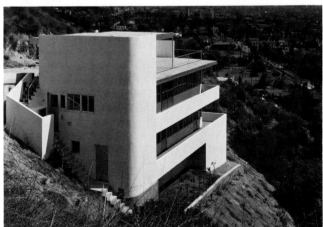

The four-story Kun house (*left*) occupies a hillside site and is entered from the top floor. Extensive balconies give each level the character of a penthouse suite. The Koblick house (*above and right*) contains two separately entered apartments, one of them a rental unit, and uses the garage as a podium for the balconies above. Both buildings exemplify Neutra's urbane response to difficult sites.

MILLER HOUSE, PALM SPRINGS, 1937

A screened porch and a reflecting pool are
the most conspicuous external features of
this small house set in a spectacular desert
landscape. The owner conducted exercise
classes according to the Mensendieck
method in the sparsely furnished studio-
living room. A sliding glass wall and panels
of translucent glass contribute to an
austere repose reminiscent of a Japanese
tea house.

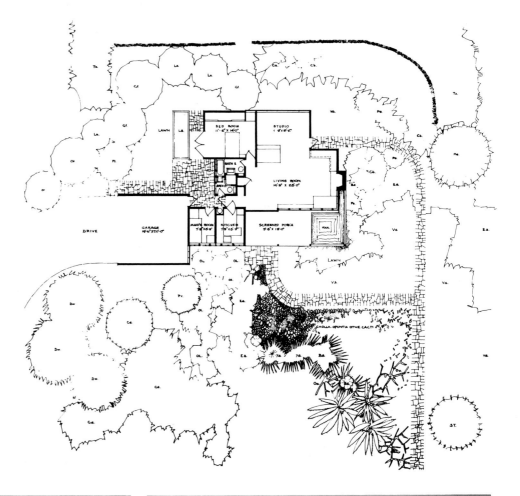

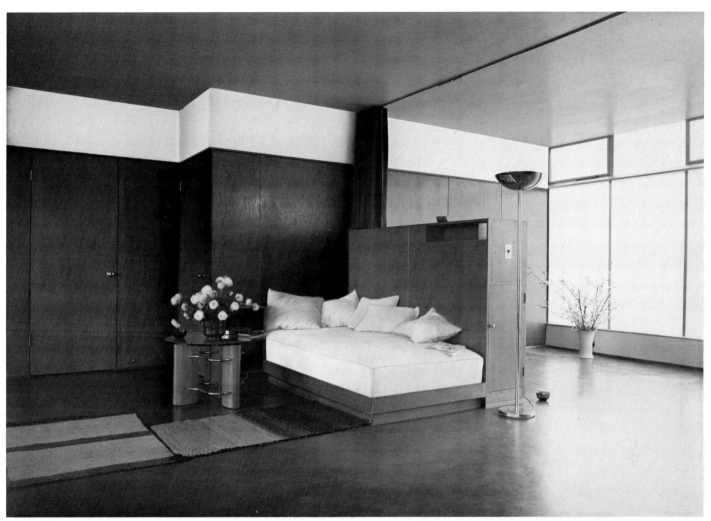

KAHN HOUSE, SAN FRANCISCO, 1940

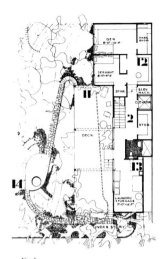

UPPER STORY

GROUND STORY

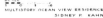
MULTISTORY OCEAN VIEW RESIDENCE
SIDNEY P. KAHN

Built on a hidden dead-end street carved out of San Francisco's Telegraph Hill, this four-story house has a spectacular view of the Embarcadero and the Bay Bridge. Living room, bar, and terrace are on the top floor and have the atmosphere of a private nightclub; dining room and kitchen are on the floor below. Open metal parapets do not block the view and make the rear elevation lighter than that of the Kun house (page 70).

LANDFAIR APARTMENTS, LOS ANGELES, 1937

Neutra's preference for frequent jogs or setbacks works to great advantage in these offset rowhouses. The site is nearly filled by an L-plan in which the long arm consists of six two-story units, each containing a four-room duplex apartment. The short stem contains one five-room apartment on each of its two floors. All kitchens have separate service entrances. Fenestration is nearly continuous and there are no visible party walls. The duplex apartments have access to roofed sun decks that vary the skyline. Compared to earlier European efforts along similar lines, these housing units are more livable and certainly more interesting architecturally.

Now operated as a private dormitory cooperative by UCLA students, the building has been altered almost beyond recognition.

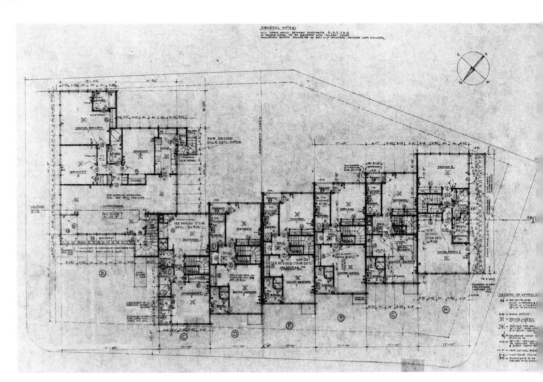

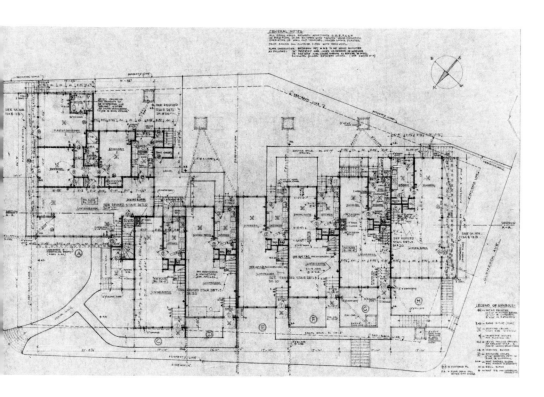

STRATHMORE APARTMENTS, LOS ANGELES, 1937

Eight apartments, each on a single floor, are divided among four separate buildings of unequal size. Grouped around a central garden court, they are well planned for maximum privacy, but as a result have fewer windows and somewhat less cramped layouts than the Landfair Apartments.

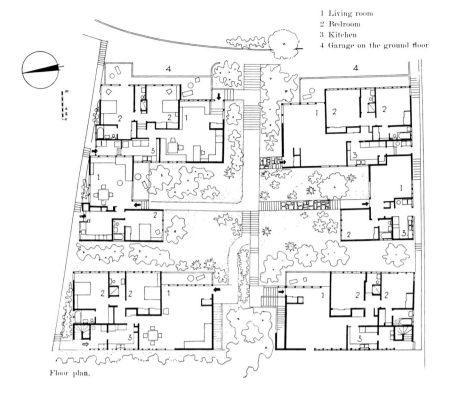

1 Living room
2 Bedroom
3 Kitchen
4 Garage on the ground floor

Floor plan.

(*At left*): Neutra and film star Louise Rainer in her Strathmore apartment.

BROWN HOUSE, FISHERS ISLAND, NEW YORK, 1938

Nothing in the design of this summer house —least of all the generous amount of glass — would suggest that it was built on a windswept site some twenty miles off New London, Connecticut. The horizontal wood siding (painted silver-gray) recalled its California origin as compared with the flush vertical siding favored by Gropius and Breuer for their New England houses of the same time. The client, John Nicholas Brown, responded to Neutra's usual questionnaire about the kind of accommodation desired with detailed answers of almost Freudian complexity. These requirements were reflected in the intricacies of the plan but not in the sleek elevations. For all its size (34 rooms) few of its interiors presented dramatic spaces. The most beautiful was the austere and decidedly Japanese corner of the music room. The building was designed within the parameters of Neutra's 1930s aesthetic and illustrates some of the problems of generating interesting elevations for a large house on a level site. Nevertheless, it was more successful than Gropius and Breuer's 1939 Frank house in Pittsburgh, which is comparable in size. The Brown house was destroyed by fire in 1975.

Second-Floor Plan

20 South terrace
21 Master bedroom
22 Mistress bedroom
23, 24 Baths
25 Guestroom
26 Hall
27 Tutor's room
28 Storage
29 Children's quarter (dividable)
30 Bath

First-Floor Plan

 1 Social activities
 2 Family quarters (dividable)
 3 Bath and toilet
 4 Entry
 5 Guestroom
 6 Screened porch
 7 Terrace
 8 Den
 9 Dining room
10 Art gallery
11 Pantry
12 Dining terrace
13 Kitchen
14 Servants' dining room
15, 16, 18 Servants' rooms
17 Bath
19 Drying area

Basement Plan

31 Storage room
32 Playroom and cinema
33, 34 Servants' rooms
35 Furnace room
36 Laundry
37 Garage

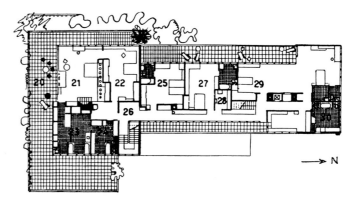

→ N

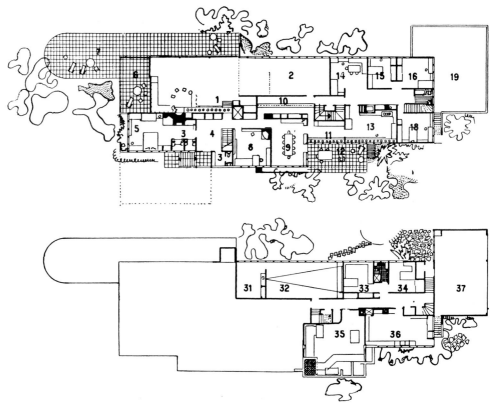

DAVEY HOUSE, MONTEREY PENINSULA, 1939

Among the first of Neutra's redwood houses, this composition retains his earlier "purist" idiom with de Stijl-like wall and roof planes that seem to bypass each other. Studio, study, and garage on the ground floor, with bedrooms above, provide a backdrop to a living room pavilion open to the view on three sides.

An extended architectural approach to a front door is unusual for Neutra. It was possible here because a separate garage, attached to guest quarters, is linked to the main house by a long brick-paved path, roofed and screened from the garden by a low brick wall. Flush wood siding, plywood, and redwood board and batten walls yield a sequence of agreeable textures, becoming more rustic as one moves through the house to the garden.

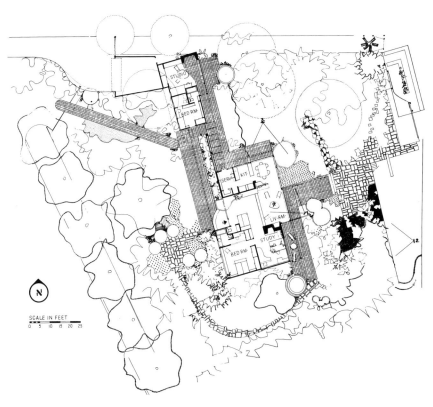

SCALE IN FEET
0 5 10 15 20 25

A shed roof terminated by a band of board and batten siding gives greater height to the garden elevations *(opposite page)* and an opportunity to vary the windows *(left)*.

BAILEY HOUSE, LOS ANGELES, 1947

Like the Nesbitt house, this building uses brick and wood but also includes a low stucco wall to screen the carport. The plan skillfully extends the living-dining frontage on the garden by including one bedroom within its range of glass walls; another bedroom is placed behind it for greater seclusion. By the forties Neutra was using large sheets of glass with few if any vertical interruptions, and the characteristic proportions become more emphatically horizontal.

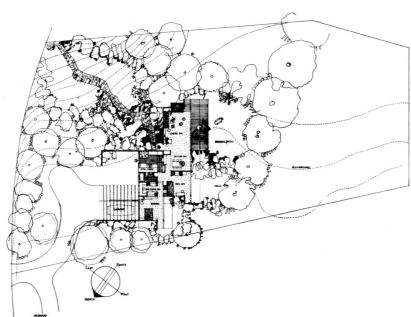

KAUFMANN HOUSE, PALM SPRINGS, 1946

This large house is brought down to pavilion scale by its pinwheel plan, which allows only two wings to be seen at one time. Stepped roofs for the living room and master bedroom areas, and a small rooftop shelter Neutra called a "gloriette," make a pyramidal composition more centrally focused than was usual for his one-story houses. Round steel columns are of minimum dimensions and the framing of glass walls is refined to the point of physical fragility, but the textures of wood and stone restore substance to an otherwise attenuated design. A semi-enclosed outdoor sitting area separates the main house from the guest wing, and the spectacular desert backdrop is reinforced by boulders scattered around the site like bushes.

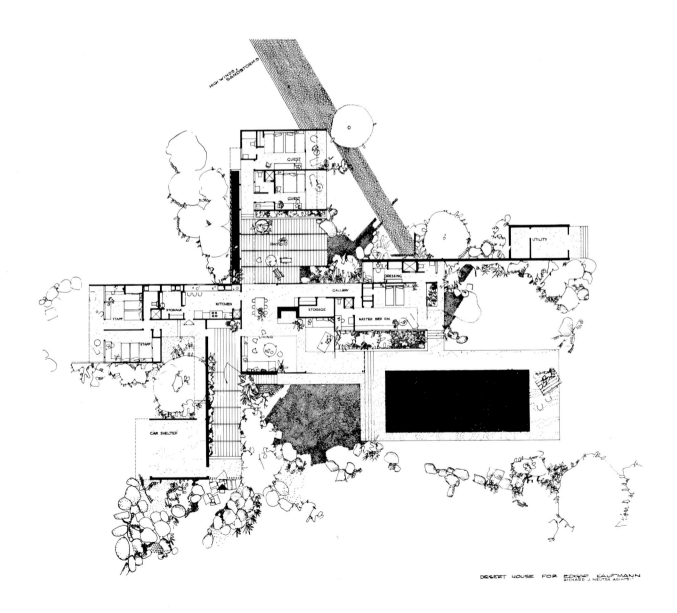

DESERT HOUSE FOR EDGAR KAUFMANN
RICHARD J NEUTRA ARCHT

Space is modulated by minor changes in ceiling heights and by sliding glass walls at the southeast corners of the living room and master bedroom. When these walls are pulled back the corner is defined only by tracks on the floors and ceilings. The spatial effect is akin to the "virtual volume" produced by some kinetic sculptures. Removal of a vertical support from its obvious location—where walls or beams intersect—to a position outside the implied space has its counterpart in classical Japanese structure, as shown on page 50.

TREMAINE HOUSE, SANTA BARBARA, 1947

The Tremaine house uses a pinwheel plan comparable to that for the Kaufmann house, but it is on a sloping site and one wing is a terrace 56 feet long and 14 feet wide, with dressing rooms beneath it adjoining a swimming pool at the downhill end. Of greater importance to the architectural character of this house is the use of reinforced concrete piers, spaced 16 feet apart on the western elevation. The piers support girders that carry cantilevered cross beams and a thin roof slab. It is a structural system that implies disciplined regularity, but the spacing of piers varies from 16 to 20 feet. They are freely moved out of alignment when they interfere with the plan; and one, in the living room, is replaced by a 6-inch-diameter steel lally column. The structural system derives from Neutra's wartime projects for Puerto Rico, but here it is visually complicated by the plan, which creates awkward intersections. The bolder scale of the structure is only partially realized, and Neutra's own response to its possibilities seems to have been ambivalent.

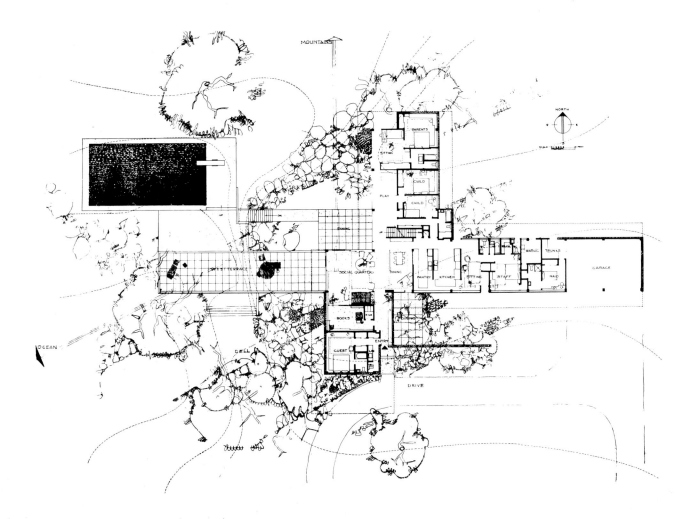

The east end of the bedroom wing is partly below grade. At the northeast corner (*below and right*) the master bedroom uses butt-jointed glass in a detail that brings the landscape quite directly into the composition.

HINDS HOUSE, LOS ANGELES, 1951

By the 1950s Neutra's less elaborate houses were designed with few sliding glass walls and with most windows fixed in place. The Hinds house has sheets of glass 12 feet long and 42 inches high without visible frames, making the interiors surprisingly open. Ventilation is through louvers at floor level. The beautifully proportioned rear elevation is tied to the site by a wall projecting from it; this element is an outdoor closet for garden tools.

Corners of butt-jointed glass, and external columns and beams making "displaced" corners, are ubiquitous features of Neutra's later houses. They are combined in the Perkins house with a free-form pool extending into the living room (*below left*). The pool side of the Moore house (*below right and opposite*) is as delicately scaled as a gazebo. Its second fascia is projected from the roof to cast a shadow, but is of greater value as an enrichment of linear detail.

PALOS VERDES HIGH SCHOOL, PALOS VERDES, CAL., 1961   with Robert Alexander

More overtly regional and "historical" than his other work of the period, this project anticipated the renewal of interest in historical allusion. Stucco walls and pitched roofs covered in red-orange tile make these school buildings look like distant relatives of California missions, although the covered walkways retain Neutra's familiar design details. The end elevations are also comparable to the farm buildings Neutra sketched on his student holidays (page 23).

PHOTOGRAPH CREDITS

Julius Shulman: Cover, 10 right, 12 top and center, 52, 53 top and bottom right, 54 top, 67 top left and right, 69 bottom, 71-75, 77-79, 86 bottom, 94-99, 101-103, 105-113

Architectural Forum: 21 bottom

Brenenstul: 50 bottom

Charles Eames: 55

Feudal Architecture of Japan by Kiyoshi Hirai. Weatherhill/Heibonsha. (New York: 1965): 50 second from top

John Hagerty: 22 top

Hedrich Blessing: 21 top

G.E. Kidder Smith: 12 bottom

Luckhaus Studio: 9 second from top, 43 top, 45 bottom, 47 bottom, 50 second from bottom, 58-61, 63 bottom, 64, 66, 67 bottom, 68, 69 top, 70, 80-84, 86 top, 87 bottom, 92, 93

Dexter Morand: 10 left

Willard D. Morgan: 43 bottom, 44

The Museum of Modern Art: 11 (Pierre Adler), 17, 18 (Kate Keller), 23-38, 39 top and center; 40, 41, 48 bottom left (Pierre Adler), 48 bottom right, 49 (George Barrows), 51 top (Arthur Drexler), 56 bottom (George Barrows)

James H. Reed: 54 bottom

© Dr. Franz Stoedtner: 7 bottom

© Ezra Stoller: 22 center and bottom; 53 bottom left